A F T E R

T H E

F U T U R E

franco "bifo" berardi

Edited by Gary Genosko and Nicholas Thoburn

AFTER

THE

FUTURE

franco "bifo" berardi

Translated by Arianna Bove, Melinda Cooper, Erik Empson, Enrico,
Giuseppina Mecchia, and Tiziana Terranova

After the Future
By Franco Berardi
Edited by Gary Genosko and Nicholas Thoburn

© 2011 Franco Berardi
Preface © 2011 Gary Genosko and Nicholas Thoburn

This edition © 2011 AK Press (Edinburgh, Oakland, Baltimore)

ISBN-13: 978-1-84935-059-4
Library of Congress Control Number: 2011920477

AK Press	AK Press UK
674-A 23rd Street	PO Box 12766
Oakland, CA 94612	Edinburgh EH8 9YE
USA	Scotland
www.akpress.org	www.akuk.com
akpress@akpress.org	ak@akedin.demon.co.uk

The above addresses would be delighted to provide you with the latest AK Press
distribution catalog, which features several thousand books, pamphlets, zines,
audio and video recordings, and gear, all published or distributed by AK Press.
Alternately, visit our websites to browse the catalog and find out
the latest news from the world of anarchist publishing:
www.akpress.org | www.akuk.com
revolutionbythebook.akpress.org

Printed in Canada with 100% union labor.
Certified by the Forest Stewardship Council.

Cover by Margaret Killjoy | www.birdsbeforethestorm.net
Interior by Kate Khatib | www.manifestor.org/design

Page 16: Photograph by Ares Ferrari, licensed under the Creative Commons Attribution-Share
Alike 3.0 Unported license.
Page 76: Photograph by The People Speak!, licensed under the Creative Commons Attribution
2.0 Generic license.
Page 128: Photograph by Mark Miller, licensed under the Creative Commons Attribution-
Share Alike 2.0 Generic license.
All other images public domain or unkown. All attempts have been made to contact the
photographers or rights holders.

Portions of this book have appeared in different form in *Precarious Rhapsody: Semiocapitalism
and the Pathologies of Post-Alpha Generation* (Minor Compositions, 2009) and *The Soul at
Work: From Alienation to Autonomy* (Semiotext(e), 2009).

CONTENTS

Chapter Four: Exhaustion and Subjectivity 121

Appendix: Interview with Franco "Bifo" Berardi 167

Bibliography 182

preface

THE TRANSVERSAL COMMUNISM OF FRANCO BERARDI

gary genosko and nicholas thoburn

WHAT HAPPENS

to political thought, practice, and imagination when it loses hold on "the future"? It goes into crisis. The analytic, psychological, and libidinal structures of twentieth-century revolutionary politics were beholden to the temporal form of the future—it even gave the first movement of the avant-garde its name: Futurism. The future was on the side of the revolution. It was a great and empowering myth, but few believe it any longer: the future is over. Its last vestiges were squandered in the schemes of a heavily futurized financial capitalism.

This is Franco Berardi's radical diagnosis. It is a *clinical* diagnosis as much as it is a political one, for Berardi traces the *symptoms* of the end of the future across the social and corporeal body. Cognitive, affective, linguistic, semiotic, desiring, economic, organizational, and mediatic processes are the matter of this assessment of the contemporary malaise. Symptoms point backwards to repressed contents, and lean into a postfuture that is still finding a way to coalesce. Such symptoms are not very enjoyable.

But the diagnosis is even more radical. The point isn't to *revive* the future in a new vanguard. The future was itself a highly suspect temporal form—for Berardi, the "imaginary effect" of the capitalist mode of production, with its expansive pursuit of surplus value. Things started to turn in 1977, the beginning of the progressive dissolution of "the century that trusted in the future." It is here identified in British punk, but also in the Italian "Movement of '77" that Berardi is so closely associated with.

Franco Berardi, or "Bifo," is principally known to Anglo-American readers for his association with *operaismo* ("workerism") and the movement of *autonomia* ("autonomy"). This current in Italian thought and extra-parliamentary politics came to prominence and considerable influence in the 1970s for its transformative approach to communist politics—placing workers' needs, desires, and organizational autonomies at the center of political praxis—and for the wave of repression unleashed against it (Wright 2002). Since then, and under the rubric of "postautonomism" and "postworkerism"—what Bifo prefers to call "compositionism"—this current has come to have considerable influence in activist circles, postmedia cultures, and the university. Antonio Negri is, of course, the principal figure here, but it would be a great mistake to take his work as an emblem for the historical forms and contemporary parameters of this mode of thought and politics as a whole.

A comrade of Negri's in the key workerist organization, Potere Operaio, Bifo's politics have continued to display the signs of the workerist current. This is not least in his insistence on engaging and researching the most contemporary technical and antagonistic *composition* of any class formation, never falling back on a preconstituted, identitarian understanding of political subjectivity. The deployment of the autonomist talisman of Marx's concept of the "general intellect" is perhaps the most enduring sign of this mode of intellectual commitment in his work. But Bifo's relation to the critical current of operaismo is something of a zigzag, a transversal connection that is as much open to the outside of autonomist politics as it is an elaboration of it.

This is no more apparent than in the Bologna collective A/Traverso ("In-between") that Bifo helped establish in the mid-1970s, and in the associated free radio station, Radio Alice. In these technocultural experiments in publishing, research, organization, and broadcasting, autonomist theses were enmeshed with pop-cultural styles, media capacities, the urban rebellions of proletarian youth, sexual politics, modernist poetics, and the conceptual innovations of poststructuralist thought, most especially those of Deleuze and Guattari. Shutdown by armed police for its contribution to the Bologna uprisings in the Spring of 1977, Radio Alice has taken on something of a mythic aspect, one confirmed in the highly evocative recent film about Radio Alice, *Lavorare con lentezza*, in which Bifo takes a cameo turn as a Marxist lawyer.

Bifo's transversal politics, writing, and media practice have since developed through numerous organizational and media forms, as radio waves have been joined by digital technologies in the field of political composition—the movement of community television, Telestreet, and the Web forum, Rekombinant, are notable instances. But returning to the themes of this book, how are Bifo's arguments different or transversal to the positions that have come to be associated with postworkerism?

Bifo's diagnosis is considerably darker than that of Hardt and Negri, as we can see with regard to the theme of "immaterial labor." In the rise to prominence of the intellectual, semiotic, and affective content of work and its product, it's now well known that Hardt and Negri detect a tendency toward workers' autonomy, where capital becomes a parasitic agent of capture *external* to the self-organization of labor. Bifo's conclusions are rather different. The agential force in contemporary configurations of work is not labor, but most decidedly *capital*. In a dozen pages of the *Grundrisse* known by operaismo as the "Fragment on Machines," Marx (1973, 692) observed that the capitalist production mechanism is a "vast automaton consisting of numerous mechanical and intellectual organs." Here, as he continues,

> Labor appears ... merely as a conscious organ, scattered among the individual living workers at numerous points of the mechanical system ... whose unity exists not in the living workers, but rather in the living (active) machinery, which confronts his individual, insignificant doings as a mighty organism. (Marx 1973, 693)

In *After the Future*, Bifo iterates Marx's thesis in the radically new times of digital capitalism. And he finds that the "automaton" has multiplied its powers to disaggregate and orchestrate the parts or organs of labor; the whole psychosphere of the human being becomes subject to the movement of capital, now operating at digital speeds. With the networking powers of information technology, the capacities of capitalist work processes to orchestrate labor have not only been extended spatially, across the globe, but have intensified temporally also. Today's firms don't purchase workers as a whole, but a fragment of their activity, sensibility, attention, communicative capacity. One of Bifo's most compelling contributions to the theory of "semiocapitalism"—capitalism that makes signs, affects, attitudes, and ideas directly productive—is the *cellularization* of labor. As production becomes semiotic, cognitive workers are precariously employed—on occasional, contractual, temporary bases—and their work involves the elaboration of segments or "semiotic artifacts" that are highly abstract entities combined and recombined through an exploitative digital network only at the precise time they are required. The social field, as he argues here, is "an ocean of valorizing cells convened in a cellular way and recombined by the subjectivity of capital." These infolaborers are paid only for the moments when their time is made cellular, yet their entire days are subjected to this kind of production, "pulsating and available, like a brain-sprawl in waiting," Blackberries and mobile phones ever ready.

The psychic and somatic form of the human cannot take this, and as our cognitive, communicative, and emotional capacities become subject to cellular fragmentation and recombination under the new machine-speed of information, we get sick. Depression, panic, unhappiness, anxiety, fear, terror—these are the affective conditions of contemporary labor, the "psycho-bombs" of cognitive capitalism, each, naturally, with its own psychopharmacology. Nonetheless, we actively submit ourselves to this regime; this is the perversity of contemporary culture. Of course, the vast majority has no choice—these are the structural conditions of work. But the progressive commercialization of culture, deadening of metropolitan life, loss of solidarity, and insidious dispersal of mechanisms of competition are such that we have come to fixate our *desires* on work. Even as it pushes human affective and cognitive capacities to breaking point, the entrepreneurial form is the only adequate expression of our current communicative and affective qualities, the one most able to confirm our increasingly competitive and narcissistic drives.

Such existential "precarity" is not to be solved by a return to the Fordist model of labor time and contract security. This was not only a temporary and now passed formation in the long history of otherwise precarious labor (and one that was even then peculiar to a particular racialized and gendered fragment of the working population). It was also the specific object of workers' resistance in the 1970s, resistance that Bifo and autonomia valorized as the "refusal of work." Neither are the militant strategies of the past any longer viable, and Bifo has no interest in reviving the corpse of orthodox communism. His opinion of this tradition is abundantly clear in *The Soul at Work*:

> The only relation between the State Communism imposed by the Leninist parties in the Soviet Union and elsewhere, and the autonomous communism of the workers, is the violence systematically exerted by the first over the second, in order to subdue, discipline, and destroy it. (Berardi 2009, 85)

There is, then, no return to Lenin or Mao. Alongside Hardt and Negri, perhaps the most prominent and influential efforts to reestablish a communism adequate to the current conjuncture are to be found in the work of Alain Badiou. In his later work, Badiou has turned away from vanguard models of the party. Yet this is because we have entered a new "sequence," beyond that which was characterized by the Leninist party form and Mao's Cultural Revolution (Badiou 2008). Bifo's difference is that, whether correctly characterized by a series of sequences or not, communism proper *never* went by the name of Lenin or Mao (the "Mao-Dadaism" of Radio Alice signified something quite other than identification with China's Great Helmsman). As shorthand for this critique, we would signal the affirmation and intensification—not refusal or overcoming—of work in the Soviet and Chinese regimes. But the problem that Bifo isolates in these pages is the *subjective political model* inherent to such orthodox communism, the "militant," and its not so distant cousin, the "activist."

Activism, Bifo argues in these pages, is the narcissistic response of the subject to the infinite and invasive power of capital, a response that can only leave the activist frustrated, humiliated, and depressed. Bifo here locates this modern political configuration in Lenin, and makes a most heretical statement: "I am convinced that the twentieth century would have been a better century had Lenin not existed." He arrives at this diagnosis through a reading of Lenin's bouts of depression, but the condition is not exclusive to Lenin. Indeed, elsewhere Bifo identifies a similar fixation in Félix Guattari, a most surprising move, given the sophistication of Guattari's schizoanalytic critique of authoritarian political subjectivation. Bifo developed his friendship with Guattari while in exile from Italy in the 1980s, a period that Guattari characterized as his "winter years," the coincidence of personal depression and neoliberal reaction. Under these conditions, a certain political activism appeared central to Guattari, but not so to Bifo: "I remember that in the 1980s Félix often scolded me because I was no longer involved in some kind of political militancy.... For me, militant will and ideological action had become impotent" (Berardi 2008, 13). For Bifo, in times of reaction, of the evacuation of political creativity from the social field, activism becomes a desperate attempt to ward off depression. But it's doomed to fail and, worse, to convert political innovation and sociality into its opposite, to "replace desire with duty":

> Félix knew this, I am sure, but he never said this much, not even to himself, and this is why he went to all these meetings with people who didn't appeal to him, talking about things that

distracted him.... And here again is the root of depression, in this impotence of political will that we haven't had the courage to admit. (Berardi 2008, 13)

We would isolate two aspects of Bifo's analysis of depression. It is a product of the "panic" induced by the sensory overload of digital capitalism, a condition of withdrawal, a disinvestment of energy from the competitive and narcissistic structures of the enterprise. And it's also a result of the loss of political composition and antagonism: "depression is born out of the dispersion of the community's immediacy. Autonomous and desiring politics was a proliferating community. When the proliferating power is lost, the social becomes the place of depression" (Berardi 2008, 13). In both manifestations, depression is a real historical experience, something that must be actively faced and engaged with—one cannot merely ward it off with appeals to militant voluntarism. We need to assess its contours, conditions, and products, to find an analytics of depression, and an adequate politics. And that is the goal of this book, a first step toward a politics after the future, and after the redundant analytic and subjective forms of which the future was made.

Bifo makes use of many resources in this venture of diagnosis and escape, traversing the Futurist aesthetics of speed, the psychic corruption of Berlusconi's mediatic empire, transrational language, senility, the dotcom bubble, the Copenhagen climate summit, the dynamics of semiocapitalism, and the possibilities of a Baroque modernity. This book begins and ends with a manifesto. The first, Marinetti's *Futurist Manifesto*, opened the century that trusted in the future. Written a century later, Bifo's *Manifesto of Post-Futurism*, is a rather different entity, a love song to the "infinity of the present." As the cognitariat reconnect with their bodies and collectivities and cast off the shackles of self-entrepreneurship, then song, poetry, and therapy freely mix into a cocktail that clears the head of any further illusions of the FUTURE.

AFTER THE FUTURE

I WROTE THIS

book in different moments and circumstances during the last decade. Its parts were therefore conceived and structured in different ways and with varying aims. Readers will not be surprised to find that these compositional features are expressed in the style of the different texts they encounter here. Recent events, like the student revolts in Athens, London, and Rome, the Arab insurrections of the first months of 2011, and the Fukushima nuclear meltdown, did not find a place in the book, but they are fully inscribed in its spirit and conception, and stand as a confirmation of the irreversible devastation of the modern values of social civilization that neoliberal dogmatism has provoked. Taken together, these processes of conception, structure, aim, and style have composed a book about the end of the future, immersed in the complex constellations of the present.

In the first chapter—"The Century that Trusted in the Future"—I retrace the history of the imagination of "the future" over the twentieth century, from the enthusiastic expectations and proclamations of the Futurists to the punk announcement of "No Future." This part, which I wrote in 2009, ranges from the *Futurist Manifesto* of 1909 to the digital Futurism of the *Wired* ideology that blossomed in the last decade of the twentieth century.

If the first chapter follows a precise outline and was written in a consecutive period of time, the second is a constellation of articles and short essays that I published during the last ten years in the midst of the movement for global justice. These have appeared previously in Rekombinant. org, Generation Online, *SubStance*, and *Occupied London*.

The third chapter is dedicated to the concept of semiocapitalism and to the emergence of a societal form where Baroque spirit, plebeian violence, and high-finance criminality commingle: Italy in the age of Berlusconi.

The fourth chapter is focused on activism and current ideas about subjectivity. I try to answer the question: how can we imagine a future of conscious collective subjectivation? How will it be possible to create a collective consciousness in the age of precariousness and the fractalization of time? How will it be possible to practice social autonomy in a world where capitalism has instituted irreversible trends of destruction?

The vertiginous zero zero decade has changed our views and our landscape in an astounding way. From the dotcom crash to September

11th 2001, from the criminal wars of the Bush administration to the near collapse of the global financial economy, the recent history of the world has been marked by shocking events and surprising reversals. For me, this decade, heralded by the uprising of Seattle, and initiated by the spreading of the counterglobalization movement, has been exciting, surprising and exhilarating—but it has finally turned sad.

By the end of the decade, notwithstanding the victory of Barack Obama in the United States, the prospect was gloomy. Corporate capitalism and neoliberalism have produced lasting damage in the material structures of the world and in the social, cultural, and nervous systems of humankind. In the century's last decade, a new movement emerged and grew fast and wide, questioning everywhere the power of capitalist corporations.

I use the word "movement" to describe a collective displacing of bodies and minds, a changing of consciousness, habits, expectations. Movement means conscious change, change accompanied by collective consciousness and collective elaboration, and struggle. Conscious. Collective. Change. This is the meaning of "movement."

From Seattle 1999 to Genoa 2001 a movement tried to stop the capitalist devastation of the very conditions of civilized life. These were the stakes, no more, no less.

Activists around the world had a simple message: if we don't stop the machine of exploitation, debt, and compulsory consumption, human cohabitation on the planet will become dismal, or impossible.

Well, ten years after Seattle, in the wake of the 2009 Copenhagen summit failure, we can state that those people were speaking the truth.

The global movement against capitalist globalization reached an impressive range and pervasiveness, but it was never able to change the daily life of society. It remained an ethical movement, not a social transformer. It could not create a process of social recomposition, it could not produce an effect of social subjectivation. Those people were silenced by President Bush, after the huge demonstrations of February 15, 2003, when many millions of people worldwide gathered in the streets against the war in Iraq.

The absence of movement is visible today, at the end of the zero zero decade: the absence of an active culture, the lack of a public sphere, the void of collective imagination, palsy of the process of subjectivation. The path to a conscious collective subject seems obstructed.

What now? A conscious collective change seems impossible at the level of daily life. Yes, I know, change is happening everyday, at a pace that we have never experienced before. What is the election of a black President in the United States if not change? But change is not happening in the sphere of social consciousness. Change happens in the spectacular sphere of politics, not in daily life—and the relationship between politics and daily life has become so tenuous, so weak, that sometimes I think that, whatever happens in politics, life will not change.

The fantastic collapse of the economy is certainly going to change things in daily life: you can bet on it. But is this change consciously elaborated? Is this connected with some conscious collective action? It isn't. This is why neoliberal fanaticism, notwithstanding its failure, is surviving and driving the agenda of the powers of the world.

The so-called counterglobalization movement, born in Seattle at the close of the century, has been a collective conscious actor, a movement of unprecedented strength and breadth. But, I repeat, it has changed nothing in the daily life of the masses; it hasn't changed the relationship between wage labor and capitalist enterprise; it hasn't changed daily relationships among precarious workers; it hasn't changed the lived conditions of migrants. It hasn't created solidarity between people in the factories, in the schools, in the cities. Neoliberal politics have failed, but social autonomy hasn't emerged.

The ethical consciousness of the insanity of neoliberal politics spread everywhere, but it did not shape affective and social relations between people. The movement remains an expression of ethical protest. It has, nonetheless, produced effects. The neoliberal ideology that was once accepted as the word of God, as a natural and indisputable truth, started to be questioned and widely denounced in the days following the Seattle riots. But the ethical demonstrations did not change the reality of social domination. Global corporations did not slow the exploitation of labor or the massive destruction of the planet's environment. Warmongers did not stop organizing and launching deadly attacks against civilian populations in Afghanistan, Iraq, Palestine, and many other parts of the world.

Why? Why did the largest demonstration in human history, the antiwar Global Action that the movement launched on February 15, 2003, fail to stop the bombing of Baghdad?

Why was conscious collective action, although massive and global, unable to change things? This is the question I've been trying to answer for the last ten years. This is the question that I am trying to answer in this book.

I'll say here, in short, that the answer is not to be found in the political strategy of the struggle, but in the structural weakness of the social fabric.

During the twentieth century, social struggle could change things in a collective and conscious way because industrial workers could maintain solidarity and unity in daily life, and so could fight and win. Autonomy was the condition of victory, because autonomy means the ability to create social solidarity in daily life, and the ability to self-organize outside the rules of labor and exploitation. Autonomous community was the condition of political strength. When social recomposition is possible, so is collective conscious change.

In social history we can speak of recomposition when the forces of labor create common cultural flows and a common ground of sensibility, so that they become a collective actor, sharing the same questions and sometimes the same answers.

In conditions of social recomposition, social autonomy from capital becomes possible. Autonomy is the possibility of meeting the power of capital, with counterpower in daily life, in factories, neighborhoods, homes, in the affective relationships between people.

That seems to be over. The organization of labor has been fragmented by the new technology, and workers' solidarity has been broken at its roots. The labor market has been globalized, but the political organization of the workers has not. The infosphere has dramatically changed and accelerated, and this is jeopardizing the very possibility of communication, empathy, and solidarity.

In the new conditions of labor and communication lies our present inability to create a common ground of understanding and a common action. The movement that spread in the first years of the decade has been able to denounce the effects of capitalist globalization, but it hasn't been able to find the new path of social organization, of autonomy from capitalist exploitation.

This book is not linear in its composition. It is an expression of the complex constellations that comprise our present. The reader may find that the development is not always perfectly consistent. Actually it is not, because I don't know where we are heading at the moment, and I don't pretend to have a solution for the current problems of social autonomy. What I can do is sketch the map of our wanderings. And search for a way out.

chapter one

THE CENTURY THAT TRUSTED IN THE FUTURE

IF WE THINK OF

the avant-garde as a conscious movement devoted to revolution in society, in communication, and in the relationship between society and communication, Futurism—namely Italian Futurism—can be considered the avant-garde's first conscious declaration. The *Futurist Manifesto* of 1909 is an act of faith in the future. I would argue that it is also the cultural and ideological inauguration of the twentieth century, *the century that trusted in the future*.

During the twentieth century Futurism, in both its Italian and Russian forms, became the leading force of *imagination* and *project*, giving birth to the language of commercial advertising (especially the Italian variation) and to the language of political agit-propaganda (the Russian variation). The idea of the future is central in the ideology and energy of the twentieth century, and in many ways it is mixed with the idea of *utopia*. Notwithstanding the horrors of the century, the utopian imagination never stopped giving new breath to the hope of a progressive future, until the high point of '68, when the *modern promise* was supposedly on the brink of fulfilment.

In the last three decades of the century, the *utopian imagination* was slowly overturned, and has been replaced by the *dystopian imagination*. For many reasons, the year 1977 can be seen as a turning point: this was the year when the punk movement exploded, whose cry—"No Future"—was a self-fulfilling prophecy that slowly enveloped the world.

A *new utopia* appeared during the last decade of the century that trusted in the future: *cyberculture*, which has given way to the imagination of a global mind, hyperconnected and infinitely powerful. This last utopia ended in depression, after the sudden shift in perspective that followed the 9/11 event, and it has finally produced a growing system of virtual life and actual death, of virtual knowledge and actual war. The artistic imagination, since that day, seems unable to escape the territory of fear and despair. Will we ever find a path beyond the limits of the *Dystopian Kingdom*?

In this book, I want to reconsider the cultural history of the century from this point of view: the mythology of the future. The future is not an obvious concept, but a cultural construction and projection. For the people of the Middle Ages, living in the sphere of a theological culture, perfection was placed in the past, in the time when God created the universe and humankind. Therefore, historical existence takes the shape of the Fall, the abandonment and forgetting of original perfection and unity.

The rise of the myth of the future is rooted in modern capitalism, in the experience of expansion of the economy and knowledge. The idea that the future will be better than the present is not a natural idea, but the imaginary effect of the peculiarity of the bourgeois production model. Since its beginning, since the discovery of the new continent and the rewriting of the maps of the world, modernity has been defined by an amplification of the very limits of the world, and the peculiarity of capitalist economy resides exactly in the accumulation of the surplus value that results in the constant enhancement of the spheres of material goods and knowledge.

In the second part of the nineteenth century, and in the first part of the twentieth, the myth of the future reached its peak, becoming something more than an implicit belief: it was a true faith, based on the concept of "progress," the ideological translation of the reality of economic growth. Political action was reframed in the light of this faith in a progressive future. Liberalism and social democracy, nationalism and communism, and anarchism itself, all the different families of modern political theory share a common certainty: notwithstanding the darkness of the present, the future will be bright.

In this book I will try to develop the idea that the future is over. As you know, this isn't a new idea. Born with punk, the slow cancellation of the future got underway in the 1970s and 1980s. Now those bizarre predictions have become true. The idea that the future has disappeared is, of course, rather whimsical—since, as I write these lines, the future hasn't stopped unfolding.

But when I say "future," I am not referring to the direction of time. I am thinking, rather, of the psychological perception, which emerged in the cultural situation of progressive modernity, the cultural expectations that were fabricated during the long period of modern civilization, reaching a peak in the years after the Second World War. Those expectations were shaped in the conceptual frameworks of an ever progressing development, albeit through different methodologies: the Hegelo-Marxist mythology of *Aufhebung* and founding of the new totality of Communism; the bourgeois mythology of a linear development of welfare and democracy; the technocratic mythology of the all-encompassing power of scientific knowledge; and so on.

My generation grew up at the peak of this mythological temporalization, and it is very difficult, maybe impossible, to get rid of it, and look at reality without this kind of cultural lens. I'll never be able to live in accordance with the new reality, no matter how evident, unmistakable, or even dazzling its social planetary trends. These trends seem to be pointing toward the dissipation of the legacy of civilization, based on the philosophy of universal rights.

The right to life, to equal opportunities for all human beings, is daily denied and trampled on in the global landscape, and Europe is no exception. The first decade of the new century has marked the obliteration of the right to life for a growing number of people, even though economic growth has enhanced the amount of available wealth and widened the consumption of goods. A growing number of people are forced to leave their villages and towns because of war, environmental waste, and famine. They are rejected, marginalized, and simultaneously subjected to a new form of slave exploitation. The massive internment of migrant workers in detention centers disseminated all over the European territory dispels the illusion that the "camp" has been wiped out from the world. Authoritarian racism is everywhere, in the security laws passed by European parliaments, in the aggressiveness of the European white majority, but also in the ethnicization of social conflicts and in Islamist fundamentalism.

The future that my generation was expecting was based on the unspoken confidence that human beings will never again be treated as Jews were treated during their German nightmare. This assumption is proving to be misleading.

I want to rewind the past evolution of the future in order to understand when and why it was trampled and drowned.

FUTURISM AND THE REVERSAL OF THE FUTURE

On Feb 20,1909 Filippo Tommaso Marinetti published the first *Futurist Manifesto*, the same year that Henry Ford launched the first assembly line in his automobile factory in Detroit. Both events inaugurated

MANIFESTO OF FUTURISM
Filippo Tommaso Marinetti

1. We want to sing the love of danger, the habit of energy and rashness.

2. The essential elements of our poetry will be courage, audacity and revolt.

3. Literature has up to now magnified pensive immobility, ecstasy and slumber. We want to exalt movements of aggression, feverish sleeplessness, the double march, the perilous leap, the slap and the blow with the fist.

4. We declare that the splendor of the world has been enriched by a new beauty: the beauty of speed. A racing automobile with its bonnet adorned with great tubes like serpents with explosive breath ... a roaring motor car which seems to run on machine-gun fire, is more beautiful than the Victory of Samothrace.

5. We want to sing the man at the wheel, the ideal axis of which crosses the earth, itself hurled along its orbit.

6. The poet must spend himself with warmth, glamour and prodigality to increase the enthusiastic fervor of the primordial elements.

7. Beauty exists only in struggle. There is no masterpiece that has not an aggressive character. Poetry must be a violent assault on the forces of the unknown, to force them to bow before man.

8. We are on the extreme promontory of the centuries! What is the use of looking behind at the moment when we must open the mysterious shutters of the impossible? Time and Space died yesterday. We are already living in the absolute, since we have already created eternal, omnipresent speed.

9. We want to glorify war—the only cure for the world—militarism, patriotism, the destructive gesture of the anarchists, the beautiful ideas which kill, and contempt for woman.

10. We want to demolish museums and libraries, fight morality, feminism and all opportunist and utilitarian cowardice.

11. We will sing of the great crowds agitated by work, pleasure and revolt; the multi-colored and polyphonic surf of revolutions in modern capitals: the nocturnal vibration of the arsenals and the workshops beneath their violent electric moons: the gluttonous railway stations devouring smoking serpents; factories suspended from the clouds by the thread of their smoke; bridges with the leap of gymnasts flung across the diabolic cutlery of sunny rivers: adventurous steamers sniffing the horizon; great-breasted locomotives, puffing on the rails like enormous steel horses with long tubes for bridle, and the gliding flight of aeroplanes whose propeller sounds like the flapping of a flag and the applause of enthusiastic crowds.

the century that trusted in the future. The assembly line is the technological system that best defines the age of industrial massification. Thanks to it, the mass production of the automobile became possible and the mobilization of social energies was submitted to the goal of the acceleration of labor's productivity.

Acceleration, speed, the cult of the machine—these are the values emphasized by the *Futurist Manifesto*. Marinetti's text is a hymn to the disrupting modernity that in those decades was changing the face of the world, especially in the industrialized countries. Italy was not one of them: having only recently achieved national unification, its economy was based on agriculture, and the Italian style of life and consumption was traditional and backward. It wasn't by chance that the Futurist movement surfaced in Italy—and in Russia. These two countries shared a common social situation: scant development of industrial production, the marginality of the bourgeois class, a reliance on cultural and religious models of the past, the allure of foreign culture (especially French) for urban intellectuals. This is the background of the Futurist explosion, both in Italy and in Russia, but we should not only see this movement as a reaction against national backwardness. On the contrary, it activated an aesthetic energy that spread all over Europe during the following decades; it was the artistic core of the enthusiastic belief that the future would fulfil great expectations in the fields of politics, science, technology, and new styles of life.

> We declare that the splendor of the world has been enriched by a new beauty: the beauty of speed. A racing automobile with its bonnet adorned with great tubes like serpents with explosive breath ... a roaring motor car which seems to run on machine-gun fire, is more beautiful than the Victory of Samothrace. (ibid.)

The *Futurist Manifesto* declared the aesthetic value of speed. The myth of speed sustained the whole edifice of modernity's imaginary, and the reality of speed played a crucial role in the history of capital, whose development is based on the acceleration of labor time. Productivity in fact is the growth rate of accumulated relative surplus value, determined by the speed of the productive gesture and the intensification of its rhythm.

We will sing of the great crowds agitated by work, pleasure and revolt; the multicolored and polyphonic surf of revolutions in modern capitals: the nocturnal vibration of the arsenals and the workshops beneath their violent electric moons: the gluttonous railway stations devouring smoking serpents; factories suspended from the clouds by the thread of their smoke; bridges with the leap of gymnasts flung across the diabolic cutlery of sunny rivers: adventurous steamers sniffing the horizon; great-breasted locomotives, puffing on the rails like enormous steel horses with long tubes for bridle, and the gliding flight of aeroplanes whose propeller sounds like the flapping of a flag and the applause of enthusiastic crowds. (ibid.)

The Manifesto asserted the aesthetic value of the machine. The machine par excellence is the speed machine, the car, the airplane, tools making possible the mobilization of the social body. Marinetti dedicated a poem to the racing car:

To The Racing Car

Veeeeehemently god of a race of steel
Car drrrunken on space,
that paws the ground and trembles with anguish
seizing the bit with shrill teeth …
Formidable Japanese monster,
with the eyes of a forge,
nourished on flame
and mineral oils,
eager for horizons and sidereal prey …
I unchain your heart that pulsates diabolically,
I unchain your gigantic tires,
for the dance that you know how to dance
away through the white sheets of the whole world!
(Marinetti 2004, 47)

For us, dwellers in the postmodern conurbation, driving back home from the office, stuck and immovable in the traffic jam of rush hour, Marinetti's adoration of the car seems a little bit ludicrous. But the reality and concept of the machine have changed, a hundred years after the *Futurist Manifesto*. Futurism exalted the machine as an external object, visible in the city landscape, but now the machine is inside us: we are no longer obsessed with the external machine; instead, the "infomachine" now intersects with the social nervous system, the "biomachine" interacts with the genetic becoming of the human organism. Digital and biotechnologies have turned the external machine of iron and steel into the internalized and recombining machine of the bio-info era. The bio-info machine is no longer separable from body or mind, because it's no longer an external tool, but an internal transformer of body and mind, a linguistic and cognitive enhancer. Now the nanomachine is mutating the human brain and the linguistic ability to produce and communicate. The machine is us.

In the mechanical era, the machine stood before the body, and changed human behavior, enhancing our potency without changing our physical structure. The assembly line, for instance, although improving and increasing the productive power of laborers did not modify their physical organism nor introduce mutations inside their cognitive ability. The machine is no longer in front of the body but inside it. Bodies and minds therefore cannot express and relate anymore without the technical support of the biomachine.

Because of this, political power has changed its nature. When the machine was external, the State had to regulate the body and for this it used the law. Agencies of repression were used to force the conscious organisms to submit to the State's rhythm without rebellion. Now political domination is internalized and indistinguishable from the machine itself. Both the machine and the machinic imagination undergo a mutation. Marinetti thought of the machine in modern terms, as an external enhancer. In the biosocial age, the machine is informational: an internalized process of linguistic modeling, logic, and cognitive automatisms.

A hundred years after the publication of the *Futurist Manifesto*, speed also has been transferred from the realm of external machines to the information domain. Speed itself has been internalized. During the twentieth century, the machine of speed accomplished the colonization of global space; this was followed by the colonization of the domain of time, of the mind and perception, so that the future collapsed. The collapse of the future is rooted in the acceleration of psychic and cognitive rhythm.

Thanks to the external machine the spatial colonization of our planet has been accomplished: transportation tools allow us to reach every inch of the Earth, and give us the possibility of knowing, marking, controlling, and exploiting every single place. The machines have made it possible to excavate at a tremendous rate, to penetrate the bowels of the Earth, to exploit underground resources, to occupy every visible spot with the products of technical reproduction. As long as spatial colonization was underway, as long as the external machine headed toward new territories, a future was conceivable, because the future is not only a dimension of time, but also of space. The future is the space we do not yet know; we have yet to discover and exploit it. Now that every inch of the planet has been colonized, the colonization of the temporal dimension has began, i.e., the colonization of mind, of perception, of life. Thus begins the century with no future.

The question of the relationship between an unlimited expansion of cyberspace and the limits of cybertime opens up here. Being the virtual intersection of the projections generated by countless users, cyberspace is unlimited and in a process of continuous expansion. Cybertime, the ability of social attention to process information in time, is organic, cultural, and emotional, therefore anything but unlimited. Subjected to the infinite acceleration of infostimuli, the mind reacts with either panic or desensitization. The concept of sensibility, and the different but related concept of sensitivity, are crucial here. Sensitivity is the ability of the human senses to process information; sensibility is the faculty that makes empathic understanding possible, the ability to comprehend what words cannot say, the power to interpret a continuum of non-discrete elements, nonverbal signs, and the flows of empathy. This faculty, which enables humans to understand ambiguous messages in the context of relationships, might now be disappearing. We are currently witnessing the development of a generation of human beings lacking competence in sensibility, the ability to empathically understand the other and decode signs that are not codified in a binary system.

When the punks cried "No Future," at the turning point of 1977, it seemed like a paradox that couldn't be taken too seriously. Actually, it was the announcement of something quite important: the perception of the future was changing. The future is not a natural dimension of the mind. It is a modality of projection and imagination, a feature of expectation and attention, and its modalities and features change with the changing of cultures. Futurism is the artistic movement that embodies and asserts the accomplished modernity of the future. The movement called Futurism announces what is most essential in the twentieth century because this century is pervaded by a religious belief in the future. We don't believe in the future in the same way. Of course, we know that a time after the present is going to come, but we don't expect that it will fulfill the promises of the present.

The Futurists—and the moderns in general—thought that the future is reliable and trustworthy. In the first part of the century, fascists and communists and the supporters of democracy held very different ideas, and followed divergent methods, but all of them shared the belief that the future will be bright, no matter how hard the present. Our postfuturist mood is based on the consciousness that the future is not going to be bright, or at least we doubt that the future means progress.

Modernity started with the reversal of the theocratic vision of time as a Fall and a distancing from the City of God. Moderns are those who live time as the sphere of a progress toward perfection, or at least toward improvement, enrichment, and rightness. Since the turning point of the century that trusted in the future—which I like to place in 1977—humankind has abandoned this illusion. The insurgents of '68 believed that they were fulfilling the modern Hegelian utopia of the becoming-true of thought, the Marcusean fusion of reason and reality. But the integration of reality and reason (embedded in social knowledge, information, and technology) turned history into a code-generated world. Terror and Code took over the social relationship and *utopia* went *dystopic*. The century that trusted in the future could be described as the systematic reversal of *utopia* into *dystopia*. Futurism chanted the utopia of technique, speed, and energy, but the result was Fascism in Italy and totalitarian Communism in Russia.

THE MEDIA UTOPIA OF THE AVANT-GARDE

Avant-garde is a word that comes from a military lexicon. Both Russian and Italian Futurisms have a military character and military conceptions of cultural action. But the word avant-garde is also linked to the concept of utopia, as it implies the opening and prefiguration of a possible historical future.

Neruda speaks of utopia in terms of an horizon. We walk and see the horizon, and in that direction we head. Although the horizon is shifting further and further and we can never reach it, looking at it gives sense to our walking. Utopia is like the horizon. The etymology of the word implies that utopia can never be brought into existence, but the history of the twentieth century avant-garde tells a different story. Generally, utopia has been realized, although in an inverted sense: the libertarian utopias of the century have generally given birth to totalitarian regimes. The utopia of the machine, nurtured by Italian Futurism, gave birth to the overproduction of cars and to the alienated production form of the assembly line. The communitarian utopia gave birth to the reality of nationalism and fascism. The utopia of Russian Futurism met the totalitarian violence of Stalinism.

Then, at the end of the century that trusted in the future, utopia gives birth to the kingdom of dystopia. In the first decades of the century, machines for the amplification and diffusion of the voice were an indispensable tool for the creation of authoritarian power. Both democratic and totalitarian regimes based the creation of consensus on the new electric technologies of communication (loudspeaker, radio, and cinema), giving leaders the possibility to fill huge urban places with crowds of followers, and to bring together wide territories and distant populations. Futurism experimented with and anticipated this utilization of the media. The biographies of artists like Marinetti, Russolo, Cangiullo, Depero and many other Italian Futurists attest to this anticipation. Emphasizing electricity as the universal medium, Futurism can be viewed as the premonition of the ultimate utopia, *cyberculture*, emerging in the last two decades of the century.

Paul Valéry writes somewhere that, in the future, the citizens of the world will be able to receive information directly in their houses, like water that comes out of the tap. The universal flow of communication was seen as the actualization of the ideal human universality. The "wireless imagination" that Marinetti speaks of is the origin of the network of technique, knowledge and sensibility that, over the course of the century, has joined the planet, turning it into an all-pervading "Global Mind," as Kevin Kelly (1994) calls it in the book *Out of Control.*

Futurism's contribution to the development of media sensibility is significant. The visual experiments of French pointillism and divisionism at the end of the nineteenth century had opened the way to cinematic technique and perception. In those years, when cinema was beginning its development, Balla's and Boccioni's works tried to experiment with visual techniques that would create a sense of movement in the motionless framework of the painting.

Henri Bergson says that cinema demonstrates a close relationship between consciousness and the technical extroversion of movement in time. For the first time in human history, cinema makes possible the re-actualization of an action that happened in the past, and gives us the possibility of coming back to the future when future has become past. In 1912, Delaunay, a pupil of Bergson, wrote in a letter to the Italian Futurists: "Your art has velocity as expression and the cinema as a tool." The *Manifesto tecnico della pittura futurista* [*Futurist Painting: Technical Manifesto*], written in 1910 and signed by Boccioni, Balla, Carrà, Severini, and Russolo (1970, 27), proclaims the idea of dynamism: "The gesture which we would reproduce on canvas shall no longer be a fixed *moment* in universal dynamism. It shall simply be the *dynamic sensation* itself."

Futurist dynamism wants to infuse painting with the perception of temporal progression, as we can see in Balla's painting *Signorina con cagnolino,* and in Boccioni's *Stati d'animo.* Futurist innovation exploits the rhythm of technomedia innovation: photography, cinema, radio. Cubo-Futurist painters try to capture the dynamic of movement by simultaneously presenting different sides of the object, anticipating the sensibility of cinema and television. Velimir Khlebnikov and Aleksei Kruchenykh sing the praises of radio as the medium of universal love and sympathy among men. After dreaming of the evolution of the media, after proclaiming the advent of universal communication and wireless imagination, in the second half of the century the avant-garde will witness the conversion of the media into tools of domination over the collective mind. But the ambiguity is there from the beginning.

In 1921, Khlebnikov (1987, 392–96) wrote an amazing paper entitled "The Radio of the Future." In it you'll find everything and its contrary. It evokes the exhilarating adventure of communication that spreads all over the planet, joining and connecting distant villages and communities, bringing words and images, and enlightening every corner of the world. But in the same words and in the same tones you can feel the prophecy of totalitarian control, of centralized state domination which annihilates freedom. *Utopia* and *dystopia* come out from Khlebnikov's imagination of the *radio*, which is simultaneously the irradiating light of love and knowledge, and the voice of almighty *power*.

In the country of Guglielmo Marconi, Futurism translates the spirit of the new medium through the idea of wireless imagination, and Khlebnikov, in the newborn Soviet Republic, sings the praises of the irradiating medium. In Russia, these are the years of civil war and massive scarcity and starvation, but the enlightened and naive spirit of the Futurist poet wandered beyond the fog and the clouds and saw the bright future of the media. The radio becomes, in Khlebnikov's words, a gigantic screen in the central plaza of every city and village, where the people can receive news and suggestions and lessons and medical instructions. In this visionary text, Khlebnikov is clearly foreseeing what we today call the Internet, the infinite connection of places without a place. And his imagination is simultaneously wildly libertarian and despondently totalitarian. His radio broadcasts colors and images thanks to a system of mirrors reflecting what is happening in a distant place. But the flow of images and words, disseminated everywhere in the country and received by the web of radio-screens, comes from a central source: the Supreme Soviet of Sciences, broadcasting every day to all the schools and villages. Khlebnikov foretells a medium that we today call television. The history of the twentieth century may be described as the struggle between the broadcast and the web, between the centralized medium of television and the proliferating medium of the Internet. The two models obviously intermingle and interact, though their philosophies are clearly distinguishable as the *utopia* and *dystopia* of the mediascape. But in the imagination of the *Futurist King of the Universe* (as Khlebnikov named himself) the two are united in the same nightmare-dream.

ZAUM AND TECHNOMAYA

Khlebnikov's poetics can be viewed as a utopian and anticipatory appreciation of the new reality of language in the age of media tech. He was the prophet of late-century cyberculture, and the utopian thinker of the mix of technology, transmentality, and psychedelics. He created the language of "*Zaum*," transmental emotional language, referring to the ability to transfer meanings without the need for any conventional linguistic symbols.

This issue was seen clearly by the Symbolist poets. Since the end of the nineteenth century, Symbolist poetics tried to overcome linguistic limits to interpersonal comprehension and looked for a form of communication freed from semantic convention. The Symbolist poetical school started from the notion of transmental language. Mallarmé sought a poetics that could transmit emotion rather than meaning. His concept of emotion should not be understood in any romantic or decadent sense. As he wrote in a letter to Cazalis in 1864, Symbolism is "une poétique trés nouvelle, qui peut peindre non la chose mais l'effet qu'elle produit." To paint, he says, not the thing, but the effect produced in the mind of the person receiving the message. His intention has little to do with any (late) romantic aura: the emotional effect Mallarmé is talking about is the transmission of mental states. Color, phoneme, image, and word are intended to act as mental change, as neurological emotion, as synesthetic telepathy.

Khlebnikov had been influenced by Symbolist poetics before joining the Futurist movement in the roaring years of the Revolution. The affinities between Symbolism and Futurism are much more interesting than their differences. Khlebnikov, who loved to travel all around Russia by train, and who loved the archaic ways of life and magical-shamanistic practices of deep, traditional Russia, wanted to create a virtually planetary language, able to be understood beyond linguistic boundaries. He called this language *Zaum*. Angelo Maria Ripellino (1978, 93) points out that "Futurism has two faces. On one side, it emphasizes technology, skyscrapers, machines; on the other side, it's moved by the troglodytes, the wild, caves, and the Stone Age; and so it opposes the sleep of a prelogic Asia to the modern European metropolitan frenzy." Here we are on ambivalent ground, open on two different sides: *Zaum* is seduced by pre-symbolic forms of communication, the original protolinguistic vocality, the language of original emotions. But at the same time, it is predisposed to imagine the possibility of a postsymbolic communication, i.e., a telepathic technology; in that sense we see Symbolism and Futurism converging toward the imagined linguistic utopias, merging archaism and Futurism.

Khlebnikov is charmed by the enchanting virtues of sounds, by phonetic *sorcellerie* [witchcraft]:

> Faith in witchery of phonemes, interest in the shamanic culture, research of a ritual language, this is the Symbolist influence: poetry is a magical action, and an oracular message. Many poems by Bal'mont, Bel'ij, Blok are conceived as means of magical action, similar to witches' balms, animal brains, snake skin, Savina leaves and belladonna or datura and so on. (Ripellino 1978, 93)

Khlebnikov turns his back on the modern European world, notwithstanding his Futuristic flirtations, preferring eternal Asia, and he dives into the "etymological night," into the deepness of a past that reaches toward imaginary origins. In this magical background he sees the possibility of a telepathic effect of transmitting meaning without the mediation of a conventional signifier, through the direct stimulation of neurological emotions corresponding to meaning.

Khlebnikov's approach leads to presymbolic communication, but this must converge with postsymbolic research, which is our task today. Khlebnikov seems to be the point of connection between the two directions. The aim of his transmental language is to find a nonconventional dimension of communication through travel against the grain in the nocturnal territory of etymologies and origins; but now we progress toward the same end through the dangerous experimentation of telepathic techniques.

Symbolist research is explicitly tied to timeless mystical quests, because mysticism knows the way to nonconventional dimensions of communication. In *Foundations of Tibetan Mysticism*, Lama Anagarika Govinda (1960, 17) says: "The essential nature of words is therefore neither exhausted by their present meaning, nor is their importance confined to their usefulness as transmitters of thoughts and ideas." Anagarika Govinda is perfectly conscious of the fact that, in this regard, Buddhist symbolism has a deep similarity with poetical symbolism, and notes: "The magic which poetry exerts upon us, is due to this quality and the rhythm combined therewith ... The birth of language was the birth of humanity. Each word was the sound-equivalent of an experience, connected with an internal or external stimulus" (1960, 17–18). The material consistency of the poetic sign (i.e. sound, rhythm, vibration) produces its efficiency and capability to create mental effects. Referring to the Tibetan tradition, Anagarika Govinda distinguishes between the word as *shabda* and the word as *mantra*. *Shabda* is the ordinary word composing common speech, the word that is able to carry signification through conventional understanding. *Mantra*, on the other hand, is the impulse that creates a mental image, the power to change mental states. "Mantra is a tool for thinking, a thing which creates a mental picture" (1960, 19). With sound, it calls forth its content into a state of immediate reality. Mantra is power, not merely speech, which the mind can contradict or evade. What mantra expresses by its sound exists, comes to pass. It is the peculiarity of the true poet that his word creates actuality, calls forth and unveils something real. Mantra is a force able to evoke images, to create and transmit mental states.

The *characteristica universalis*, as Leibniz calls it, or translinguistic symbolization, opens an issue of great importance today, in the age of intercultural planetary communication. Poetical and magical symbolism are both involved in the process of evocation that the word and the sign can produce. But we must reconsider the problem starting from a new datum, coming from electronic technology: the virtual reality machine, which involves the same problem posed by poetical and magical symbolism, that is, the problem of telepathic communication.

Linguistic communication is made possible by signs conventionally and arbitrarily connected with meanings; here we speak of communication stimulating mental states corresponding to the image, to the emotion, to the concept that the sender wants to transmit. The production of technical tools for simulation, and especially of machines for virtual reality, puts the problem in a new light. We may label *virtual reality* any technology capable of directly transmitting impulses from one brain to another, in order to stimulate in the receiver brain a synaptic connection corresponding to a certain representation, to a certain configuration, image, concept, emotion. In a purely abstract way, we may say that virtual reality is the stimulation of a neuronic wave, structured following models that are intentional and isomorphic to the mental states corresponding to a certain experience. We can say that this technology is the most apt for a telepathic sort of communication. Jaron Lanier, who in the 1980s was the first creator of virtual reality machines, spoke in those years of postsymbolic communication. If you can provide a reality with virtual reality tools, and if you can share this reality with other persons, you no longer need to describe the world, because you can simply create this contingence, this coincidence; you don't need to describe an action, you can create it.

Starting from this premise, we can go back to the problem posed by Leibniz, the problem of *characteristica universalis*, i.e., in contemporary terms, the problem of a planetary language, of a language that should be able to connect people belonging to different cultural and linguistic traditions. Pierre Lévy (1991) has proposed in *L'idéographie dynamique* the idea of a communication technology he calls "dynamic ideography." What does it mean, synthetically? Dynamic ideography is a communication technology that enables people to transmit mental states, images, emotions, concepts, sense configurations, without any conventional means. The transmission is made possible by a direct stimulation of the neurophysical connections corresponding to sense configurations. Dynamic ideography is a communication technology that can transfer, from one communicating person to another, the mental models involved in seeing a certain image, in experiencing a certain situation, in thinking a certain concept. It's easy to see the relationship between virtual reality and dynamic ideography. Dynamic ideography is a technique that activates a sequence of virtual realities, corresponding to the contents that I want to send and communicate, an analogical tool of a global and synesthetic kind, directly acting on imagination.

Imagination is an infinite variety of analogical combinatory items, an infinite variety of possibilities that the mind processes, starting from disposable engrams. Memory storage is limited, but the possibilities of rearranging the items stored in memory are not. The process of combining these analogical plastic items is called *imagination*. The theoretical and practical study of the Becoming of Imagination can be called *psychedelics*.

"Psychedelics" is the possibility of manipulating and transforming mental activity through chemical, electrical, or other stimulation. Starting from the possibility of transmitting mental models, to stimulate synaptic waves corresponding to the mental states that we want to communicate, it is possible to share imaginary words, in mental co-evolution. On this basis, we can say that language itself is the transmission of signs intended to trigger in the mind of the receiver the building of mental models that correspond to the intentions of the sender.

In the pages of *Neuromancer*, William Gibson (1984, 81) sees the world as "cyberspace": "A consensual hallucination experienced daily by billions of legitimate operators, in every nation, by children being taught mathematical concepts.... A graphic representation of data abstracted from the banks of every computer in the human system."

Cyberspace is a hypothesis of the world: Ontology and Gnoseology are on the same level of consistency, since Being is essentially a projection. "We are in a sort of cave, like Plato said, and they're showing us endless funky films," says Philip K. Dick (in Williams 1986, 72). We can think that reality is the infinite projection of endless movies on the screen of our brain. But, if we want to move from the hallucinatory to the real-world dimension, we simply must introduce the notion of communication, i.e. sharing the hallucination. Dick continues:

> If two people dream the same dream it ceases to be an illusion; the basic test that distinguishes reality from hallucination is the *consensus gentium*, that one other or several others see it too. This is *idios kosmos*, the private dream, opposed to the shared dream of us all, the *koinos kosmos*. What is new in our time is that we are beginning to see the plastic, trembling quality of the *koinos kosmos*—which scares us, its insubstantiality—and the more-than-mere-vapor quality of the hallucination. Like SF, a third reality is formed halfway between. (in Williams 1986, 170)

The Hindus call it "*Maya*." But the concept isn't easy to understand in its deepest meaning. Maya is illusion because it has been torn from its living connections and is limited in time and space. The individuality and corporality of the unenlightened human being, trying to maintain and preserve its illusory selfhood, is Maya in this negative sense.

The body of the Enlightened One is also Maya, but not in the negative sense, because it is the conscious creation of a mind that is free from illusion. Maya does not mean illusion, but something more: I would say that it means the projection of the world. The projection of the world can be frozen and become mere illusion, self-deception, if we think that the imagined world is independent from imagination, and if we think that the imaging self is independent from communication and from the becoming of the world. But Maya in itself means projecting action, the creation of the world. Thus Maya becomes the cause of illusion, but it is not illusion itself.

We are witnessing a proliferation of technological tools for simulation. The social technology of communication is aimed at connecting the imaginations and projections of individuals and groups. This projection-web could be called *Technomaya*, neurotelematic network endlessly projecting a movie shared by all the conscious organisms who are connected. This techno-imagination, this mutual implication in the *koinos kosmos*, is socialization itself. Through the proliferation of machines for electronic, holographic, and programmed neurostimulation, we can enter the domain of Technomaya, because we can produce worlds of meaning, and we can transmit these worlds, triggering the imaginations of other people.

ACTIVISM

Futurism and the avant-garde set themselves the task of violating rules. *Deregulation* was the legacy left by Rimbaud to the experimentation of the 1900s. Deregulation was also the rallying cry of the hypercapitalism of late modernity, paving the way for the development of semiocapital. In the totalitarian period of the external machine and mechanical speed, having previously used the state form to impose its rule on society, capitalism decided to do without state mediation as the techniques of recombination and the absolute speed of electronics made it possible for control to be interiorized. In the classical form of manufacturing capitalism, price, wages, and profit fluctuations were based on the relationship between necessary labor time and the determination of value. Following the introduction of microelectronic technologies and the resulting intellectualization of productive labor, the relationship between different magnitudes of value and different productive forces entered a period of indeterminacy. Deregulation, as launched by Margaret Thatcher and Ronald Reagan, marked the end of the law of value and turned its demise into a political economy. In his major work, *Symbolic Exchange and Death*, Jean Baudrillard (1993a: 2) intuitively infers the overall direction of the development of the end of the millennium: "The reality principle corresponded to a certain stage of the law of value. Today, the whole system is swamped by indeterminacy, and every reality is absorbed by the hyperreality of the code and simulation."

The whole system precipitates into indeterminacy as all corre-spondences between symbol and referent, simulation and event, value and labor time no longer hold. But isn't this also what the avant-garde aspired to? Doesn't experimental art wish to sever the link between symbol and referent? In saying this, I'm not accusing the avant-garde of being the cause of neoliberal economic deregulation. Rather, I'm suggesting that the anarchic utopia of the avant-garde was actualized and turned into its opposite the moment society internalized rules and capital was able to abdicate both juridical law and political rationality to abandon itself to the seeming anarchy of internalized automatisms, which is actually the most rigid form of totalitarianism.

As industrial discipline dwindled, individuals found themselves in a state of ostensible freedom. No law forced them to put up with du-ties and dependence. Obligations became internalized and social con-trol was exercised through a voluntary, albeit inevitable, subjugation to chains of automatisms.

In a regime of aleatory and fluctuating values, precariousness be-came the generalized form of social relations, which deeply affected so-cial composition and the psychic, relational and linguistic characters of a new generation as it entered the labor market. Rather than a particu-lar form of productive relations, precariousness is the dark soul of the productive process. An uninterrupted flow of fractal and recombining infolabor circulates in the global web as the agent of universal valoriza-tion, yet its value is indeterminable. Connectivity and precariousness are two sides of the same coin: the flow of semiocapitalist production captures and connects cellularized fragments of depersonalized time; capital purchases fractals of human time and recombines them in the web. From the standpoint of capitalist valorization, this flow is unin-terrupted and finds its unity in the object produced; however, from the standpoint of cognitive workers the supply of labor is fragmented: frac-tals of time and pulsating cells of labor are switched on and off in the large control room of global production. Therefore the supply of labor time can be disconnected from the physical and juridical person of the worker. Social labor time becomes an ocean of valorizing cells that can be summoned and recombined in accordance with the needs of capital.

Let us return to the *Futurist Manifesto*. War and the contempt for women are the essential features of mobilization, which traverses the whole parable of historical vanguards. The Futurist ambition really consisted in mobilizing social energies toward the acceleration of the social machine's productivity. Art aided the discourse of advertising as the latter fed into mobilization. When industrial capitalism transposed into the new form of semiocapitalism, it first and foremost mobilized the psychic energy of society, bending it to the drive of competition and cognitive productivity. The *new economy* of the 1990s was essentially a *prozac economy*, both neuromobilization and compulsory creativity.

Paul Virilio has shown the connection between war and speed: in the modern forms of domination, the imposition of war onto the whole of social life is an implicit one precisely because economic competitiveness is war, and war and the economy share the common denominator of speed. As Walter Benjamin (1992, 234) writes: "all efforts to render politics aesthetic culminate in one thing: war." The aestheticization of life is one aspect of this mobilization of social energies. The aestheticization of war is functional to the subjugation of everyday life to the rule of history. War forces the global masses to partake in the process of self-realization of the Hegelian Spirit, or, perhaps more realistically, to become part of capitalist global accumulation. Captured in the dynamics of war, everyday life is ready to be subjected to the unlimited rule of the commodity.

From this standpoint, there is no difference between fascism, communism, and democracy: art functions as the element of aestheticization and mobilization of everyday life. Total mobilization is terror, and terror is the ideal condition for a full realization of the capitalist plan to mobilise psychic energy. The close relation between Futurism and *advertising* is an integral part of this process.

In *Art and Revolution: Transversal Activism in the Long Twentieth Century*, Gerald Raunig (2007) writes on the relationship between the artistic avant-garde and activism. His work provides a useful phenomenological account of the relation between art and political mobilization in the twentieth century, but it fails to grasp the absolute specificity of the current situation, that is, the crisis and exhaustion of all activism.

The term "activism" became largely influential as a result of the antiglobalization movement, which used it to describe its political communication and the connection between art and communicative action. However, this definition is a mark of its attachment to the past and its inability to free itself from the conceptual frame of reference it inherited from the twentieth century. Should we not free ourselves from the thirst for activism that led the twentieth century to the point of catastrophe and war? Shouldn't we set ourselves free from the repeated and failed attempt to act for the liberation of human energies from the rule of capital? Isn't the path toward the autonomy of the social from economic and military mobilization only possible through a withdrawal into inactivity, silence, and passive sabotage?

I believe that there is a profound relationship between the drive to activism and male depression in late modernity, which is most evident in the voluntarist and subjectivist organization of Leninism. Both from the standpoint of the history of the workers' movement in the 1900s and from that of the strategic autonomy of society from capital, I'm convinced that the twentieth century would have been a better century had Lenin not existed. Lenin's vision interprets a deep trend in the configuration of the psyche of modern masculinity. Male narcissism was confronted with the infinite power of capital and emerged from it frustrated, humiliated, and depressed. It seems to me that Lenin's depression is a crucial element for understanding the role his thought played in the development of the politics of late modernity.

I have read Hélène Carrère D'Encausse's biography of Lenin. The author is a researcher of Georgian descent, who also published *L'Empire éclaté*, where she foresaw the collapse of the Soviet empire as an effect of the insurgence of Islamic fundamentalism. What interested me in Carrère D'Encausse's biography of Lenin, more than the history of Lenin's political activity, was his personal life, his fragile psyche, and his affectionate and intellectual relationships with the women close to him: his mother, his sister, Krupskaia, comrade and wife, who looked after him at times of acute psychological crises, and, finally, Inessa Armand, the perturbing, the *unheimlich,* the lover whom Lenin cut out, along with symphonic music, for softening his character.

The psyche described in this biography is framed by depression, and Lenin's most acute crises coincided with important political shifts in the revolutionary movement. As Carrère D'Encausse writes:

> Lenin used to invest everything he did with perseverance, tenaciousness and an exceptional concentration: such consistency, which he thought necessary in each of his efforts, put him in a position of great superiority over the people around him [...]. This feature of his character often had negative effects.

Exceedingly intensive efforts would tire him and wear down his already fragile nervous system. The first crisis dates back to 1902. (Carrère D'Encausse 1998, 78)

These were the years of the Bolshevik turn, of *What Is to Be Done?* Krupskaia played a fundamental role in her comrade's crisis: she intervened to filter his relations with the outside world, paid for his therapy and isolation in clinics in Switzerland and Finland. Lenin emerged from the 1902 crisis by writing *What Is to Be Done?* and engaging in the construction of a "nucleus of steel," a block of will capable of breaking the weakest link in the (imperialist) chain. The second crisis came in 1914 at the height of the break up of the Second International and the split of the Communists. The third crisis, as you might guess, occurred in the spring of 1917. Krupskaia found a safe resort in Finland, where Lenin conceived *The April Theses* and decided to impose will on intelligence: a rupture that disregarded the deep dynamics of class struggle and forced onto them an external design. Intelligence is depressive, therefore, will is the only cure for the abyss: ignore but do not remove it. The abyss remained and subsequent years did not simply uncover it: the century slipped into it.

I don't intend to discuss the politics of Lenin's fundamental choices. I'm interested in pointing out a relationship between Bolshevik voluntarism and the male inability to accept depression and transform it from within. Here lies the root of the subjectivist voluntarism that crippled social autonomy in the 1900s. Leninism's intellectual decisions were so powerful because they papered over depression with an obsessive male voluntarism.

CONNECTION AND SENSIBILITY

By the beginning of the twenty-first century, the long history of the artistic avant-garde was over. Beginning with Wagner's *Gesamtkunstwerk* and resulting in the Dadaist cry to "*Abolish art, abolish everyday life, abolish the separation between art and everyday life,*" the history of the avant-garde culminates in the gesture of 9/11. Stockhausen had the courage to say this, although many of us were thinking the same: it was the consumate work of art of the century with no future. The fusion of art and life (or death, what difference does it make?) is clearly visible in a form of action we might call "terrorizing suicide." Let us take Pekka-Eric Auvinen as an example. The Finnish youngster turned up at his school with a machine gun, killing eight people, himself included. Printed on his T-shirt was the sentence: "Humanity is overrated." Wasn't his gesture pregnant with signs typical of the communicative action of the arts?

Let me explain: I'm not inviting the young readers of this book to go to a crowded place with an explosive belt. I'm trying to say, pay attention: a gigantic wave of desperation could soon turn into a suicidal epidemic that will turn the first connective generation into a devastating psychic bomb.

I don't think this wave of suicides can be explained in terms of morality, family values, and the weak discourse conservative thought uses to account for the ethical drift produced by capitalism. To understand our contemporary form of ethical shipwreck, we need to reflect on the transformations of activity and labor, the subsumption of mental time under the competitive realm of productivity; we have to understand the mutation of the cognitive and psychosocial system.

The context of my understanding of present historical and cultural dynamics is the transition from a realm of conjunction to one of connection, with a special focus on the emergence of the first connective generation, those who learn more words from a machine than a mother. In this transition, a mutation of the conscious organism is taking place: to render this organism compatible with a connective environment, our cognitive system needs to be reformatted. This appears to generate a dulling of the faculties of conjunction that had hitherto characterized the human condition.

The realm of sensibility is involved in this ongoing process of cognitive reformatting. Aesthetic, ethical, and political thought is reshaping its observational standpoint and framework around the passage from a conjunctive to a connective form of human concatenation.

Conjunction is becoming-other. In contrast, in connection each element remains distinct and interacts only functionally. Singularities change when they conjoin; they become something other than they were before their conjunction. Love changes the lover and a combination of a-signifying signs gives rise to the emergence of a meaning that hadn't existed prior to it. Rather than a fusion of segments, connection entails a simple effect of machinic functionality. In order to connect, segments must be compatible and open to interfacing and interoperability. Connection requires these segments to be linguistically compatible. In fact the digital web spreads and expands by progressively reducing more and more elements to a format, a standard and a code that make different segments compatible.

The segments that enter this rhizome belong to different realms of nature: they are electronic, semiotic, machinic, biological, and psychic; fibre optic circuits, mathematical abstractions, electromagnetic waves, human eyes, neurons, and synapses. The process whereby they become compatible traverses heterogeneous fields of being and folds them onto a principle of connectivity. The present mutation occurs in this transition from conjunction to connection, a paradigm of exchange between conscious organisms.

Central to this mutation is the insertion of the electronic into the organic, the proliferation of artificial devices in the organic universe, in the body, in communication, and in society. Therefore, the relationship between consciousness and sensibility is transformed and the exchange of signs undergoes a process of increasing desensitization.

Conjunction is the meeting and fusion of rounded and irregular forms that infuse in a manner that is imprecise, unrepeatable, imperfect, and continuous. Connection is the punctual and repeatable interaction of algorithmic functions, straight lines and points that juxtapose perfectly and are inserted and removed in discrete modes of interaction. These discrete modes make different parts compatible to predetermined standards. The digitalization of communication processes leads, on one hand, to a sort of desensitization to the sinuous, to the continuous flows of slow becoming, and on the other hand, to becoming sensitive to the code, to sudden changes of states, and to the sequence of discrete signs.

Interpretation follows semantic criteria in the realm of conjunction: the meaning of the signs sent by the other as she enters into conjunction with you needs to be understood by tracing the intention, the context, the nuances, and the unsaid, if necessary. The interpretative criteria of the realm of connection on the other hand are purely syntactic. In connection, the interpreter must recognise a sequence and be able to perform the operation required by general syntax or the operating system; there is no room for margins of ambiguity in the exchange of messages, nor can the intention be shown by means of nuances.

This mutation produces painful effects in the conscious organism and we read them through the categories of psychopathology: dyslexia, anxiety and apathy, panic, depression, and a sort of suicidal epidemic are spreading. However, a purely psychopathological account fails to capture the question in its depth, because we are in fact confronted with the effort of the conscious organism to adapt to a changed environment, with a readjustment of the cognitive system to the techno-communicative environment. This generates pathologies of the psychic sphere and in social relations.

Aesthetic perception—here properly conceived of as the realm of sensibility and aesthesia—is directly involved in this transformation: in its attempt to efficiently interface with the connective environment, the conscious organism appears to increasingly inhibit what we call sensibility. By sensibility, I mean the faculty that enables human beings to interpret signs that are not verbal nor can be made so, the ability to understand what cannot be expressed in forms that have a finite syntax. This faculty reveals itself to be useless and even damaging in an integrated connective system. Sensibility slows down processes of interpretation and renders them aleatory and ambiguous, thus reducing the competitive efficiency of the semiotic agent.

The ethical realm where voluntary action is possible also plays an essential role in the reformatting of the cognitive system. Religious sociologists and journalists lament a sort of ethical lack of sensitivity and a general indifference in the behavior of the new generation. In many cases, they lament the decline of ideological values or community links. However, in order to understand the discomfort that invests the ethical and political realms, the emphasis needs to be placed on aesthetics. Ethical paralysis and the inability to ethically govern individual and collective life seem to stem from a discomfort in aesthesia—the perception of the other and the self.

The arts of the 1900s favored two utopic registers: the radical utopia of Mayakovsky and the functional utopia of the Bauhaus. The dystopian thread remained hidden in the folds of the artistic and literary imagination, in Fritz Lang, expressionism, and a kind of bitter paranoid surrealism from Salvador Dali to Philip K. Dick. In the second half of the twentieth century, the literary dystopias of Orwell, Burroughs and DeLillo flourished. Only today, at the beginning of the twenty-first century, does dystopia take center stage and conquer the whole field of artistic imagination, thus drawing the narrative horizon of the century with no future. In the expression of contemporary poetry, in cinema, video-art, and novels, the marks of an epidemic of psychopathology proliferate.

In her videos, Eija-Liisa Ahtila—*Wind, If 6 was 9, Anne, Aki and God*—narrates the psychopathology of relations, the inability to touch and to be touched. In the film *Me and You and Everyone We Know*, Miranda July tells the story of a video-artist who falls in love with a young man and of the difficulty of translating emotion into words and words into touch. Language is severed from affectivity. Language and sex diverge in everyday life. Sex is talked about everywhere, but sex never speaks. Pills accelerate erections because the time for caresses is limited.

A film by Jia Zhang-Ke, entitled *Still Life* and produced in Hong Kong in 2006, shows devastation unfolding. This film is extraordinarily beautiful and tells a simple story, with the background of a sad, desolate and devastated China, as both its scenery and its soul. The predominant color is a rotten, greyish, violet green. Huo Sanming returns to his place of birth in the hope of finding his wife and daughter, whom he had left years earlier to go and find work in a distant northern mine. His village, along the riverbank of the Yangtze, no longer exists. The construction of the Three Gorges Dam had erased many villages. Houses, people, and streets were covered by water. As the building of the dam proceeds, the destruction of villages continues and the water keeps rising. Huo Sanming arrives in this scenario of devastation and rising water and is unable to find his wife and daughter; so his search begins. He looks for them as groups of workers armed with their picks take walls down, as explosives demolish buildings in the urban center. After long searches, he finally finds his wife, she has aged and been sold by her brother to another man. They meet in the rooms of a building as it's being demolished and talk about their daughter in whispers, with their heads down, against an alien architecture of bricks and iron arrayed against a shit-colored sky. In the last scene of *Still Life*, a tight-rope walker walks on a rope from the roof of a house toward nothingness, against a background that recalls the dark surrealism of Dali's bitter canvases. *Still life* is a lyrical account of Chinese capitalism, acted inside out, from the standpoint of submerged life.

In *The Corrections*, Jonathan Franzen (2001) speaks of psychopharmacological adjustments as the corrections a humanity devastated by depression and anxiety uses to adjust to an existence of mandatory feigned happiness. Corrections are the adjustments to a volatile stock market to avoid losing private pension fund investments that might suddenly disappear. Franzen recounts the old age of a father and mother from the Midwest who have gone nuts as a result of decades of hyperlabor and conformism. Corrections are small and unstoppable slides toward the point of shutting down, the horror of old age in the civilization of competition; the horror of sexuality in the world of puritan efficiency.

Franzen digs deep into the folds of the American psyche and describes in minute detail the pulpifaction of the American brain: the depression and dementia resulting from a prolonged exposure to the psychic bombardment of stress from work; apathy, paranoia, puritan hypocrisy, and the pharmaceutical industry around them; the psychic unmaking of men encapsulated in the claustrophobic shell of economic hyperprotectionism; the infantilism of people who pretend to believe, or perhaps really believe, in the fulsome Christmas fairy tale of compassionately liberal cruelty. By the end of the long awaited Christmas dinner, as the psychopathic family happily gathers together, the father tries to commit suicide by shooting himself in the mouth. He isn't successful.

Yakizakana no Uta, an animated film by Yusuke Sakamoto, starts with a fish in cellophane wrapping on a supermarket shelf. A boy grabs it and takes it to the till; he pays, leaves, puts it in the bicycle basket and cycles home. "Good morning Mr Student, I'm very happy to be with you. Don't worry, I'm not a fish who complains," the fish says while the student briskly pedals home. "It's nice to make the acquaintance of a human being. You are extraordinary beings; you are almost the masters of the universe. Unfortunately you are not always peaceful, I would like to live in a peaceful world where everyone loves one another and even fish and humans shake hands. Oh it's so nice to see the sunset, I like it ever so much," the fish becomes emotional and jumps in the cellophane bag inside the basket. "I can hear the sound of a stream…. I love the sound of streams, it reminds me of something from my childhood."

When they get home the boy unpacks the fish and puts it on a plate, throws a little salt on it, as the fish gets excited and says "Ah! I like salt very much, it reminds me of something." The boy puts it on the grill in the oven and turns the knob. The fish keeps chatting: "Oh Mr Student it's nice here, I can see a light down there … I feel hot … hot …" until its voice becomes hesitant. It starts singing a song, more and more feebly and disconnectedly, like the computer Hal in *2001: A Space Odyssey* as his wires are unplugged.

Yakizakana no Uta was perhaps the most harrowing animated film I saw in June 2006 at the Caixa Forum of Barcelona, during the *Historias animadas* festival. Yet I perceived a common tone running through all of the works presented at the festival: one of ironic cynicism, if you'll allow me this expression. *Place in Time* by Miguel Soares recounts millions of years from the standpoint of an improbable bug, an organic insect, as the world changes around it. *Animales de compañia* by Ruth Gomez uses ferocious images to tell the story of a generation of well dressed cannibals, young beasts in ties; they run and run to avoid being caught by fellows, colleagues, friends, and lovers who wound, kill, and eat them as soon as they fall, with terrified smiles and dilated eyes, into their grip.

This art is no denunciation. The terms "denunciation" and "engagement" no longer have meaning when you are a fish getting ready to be cooked. The art of the twenty-first century no longer has that kind of energy, even though it keeps using expressions from the 1900s, perhaps out of modesty, perhaps because it's scared of its own truth. Artists no longer search for a rupture, and how could they? They seek a path that leads to a state of equilibrium between irony and cynicism, that allows them to delay the execution, at least for a moment. All energy has moved to the war front. Artistic sensibility registers this shift and is incapable of opposing it. Is art simply postponement of the holocaust?

END OF THE FUTURE

The publication of the Club of Rome's book, *The Limits to Growth*, in 1972, by Donella Meadows, Dennis Meadows, Jorgen Randers, and William Behrens, marked an important step in the reversal of the progressive vision of the future. Although harshly criticized by many economists at the time, the book announced the surfacing of a consciousness of exhaustibility.

Exhaustion plays no role in the imagination of modernity, and remains unthinkable in the first part of the century that trusted in the future. But in the 1970s, underground cultural currents started to signal the new horizon of exhaustion.

In 1971 Nicholas Georgescu-Roegen, professor of Statistics and Economics in Bucharest and Paris, published *The Entropy Law and the Economic Process*; his idea of a dissipation of productive energy is a useful addition to the Marxist critique of capitalism, although Marxist philosophers have never spoken of entropy as one of the causes of the *Zusammenbruch* (breakdown) of capitalism.

In the short text "Energy and Economic Myths," published in 1975, Georgescu-Roegen writes:

The favorite thesis of standard and Marxist economists alike, however, is that the power of technology is without limits. We will always be able not only to find a substitute for a resource which has become scarce, but also to increase the *productivity* of any kind of energy and material. Should we run out of some resources, we will always think up something, just as we have continuously done since the time of Pericles. Nothing, therefore, could ever stand in the way of an increasingly happier existence of the human species. One can hardly think of a more blunt form of linear thinking. By the same logic, no healthy young human should ever become afflicted with rheumatism or any other old-age ailments; nor should he ever die. Dinosaurs, just before they disappeared from this very same planet, had behind them not less than one hundred and fifty million years of truly prosperous existence. (And they did not pollute environment with industrial waste!) (Georgescu-Roegen 1975, 360)

Georgescu-Roegen's approach is especially interesting because he points to the relationship between economic and biological dimensions:

man's addiction to exosomatic instruments ... is neither only biological nor only economic. It is bioeconomic. Its broad contours depend on the multiple asymmetries existing among the three sources of low entropy which together constitute mankind's dowry—the free energy received from the sun, on the one hand, and the free energy and the ordered material structures stored in the bowels of the earth, on the other. (Georgescu-Roegen 1975, 369)

Understanding that the economic process takes place in the sphere of life, and interferes with it, the Romanian understands that the main problem of the capitalist future is not so much the social contradiction, but the effects of economic expansion on the biosphere itself.

In the Marxist account of capitalism there is no place for the concept of limits to growth. Marx does not deal with size, only with relationships. He does not care about the possibility of exhaustion. Marx's vision of the future is focused on the idea of deployment of the inner potency of labor, and this potency is boundless, as the physical force of human work meets with the potency of the "general intellect."

But experience is showing that the deployment of the potency of labor, in its conjunction with the profit-oriented dynamics of capital, is leading to exhaustion of the planet's physical resources (air, land, water, energy sources) as well as the psychic resources of the human brain.

The 1970s were the watershed. During those years, the perception of the future shifted and, in my memory, the turning point can be dated to 1977.

Let's see why.

In 1973, Syria and Egypt launched a military operation against Israel, and a war followed. The effects of the war were resented all over the world. Oil prices went crazy. The western economy was hit harshly, and this led to recession and crisis with unemployment rising everywhere. The western governments were forced to declare a period of austerity, and people were asked to sacrifice for the sake of the economy. Inflation, stagflation, and social unrest spread all over.

For the first time in the history of capitalism, scarcity of a special resource (whether natural or man-made does not matter) became the main factor of economic crisis and social unrest. In 1977, in places like Italy and Great Britain, this social instability was the incubator of a new cultural sensibility: political activism, social movement, and artistic experimentation melted together in the cultural movements of autonomia, punk, and new wave.

The year 1977 is generally recorded as a year of violence.

In Germany, 1977 was a very gloomy year. Hans Martin Schleyer, an important corporate figure, was kidnapped and killed by the Red Army Faction, and some days later, Andreas Baader, Carl Hans Raspe, and Gudrun Ensslin died in their prison cells in Stammheim, possibly killed by the guards.

Germany in Autumn (1978), the impressive movie directed by Alf Brustellin, Rainer Werner Fassbinder, Alexander Kluge, Volker Schlöndorff and others, tells of the widespread perception of the coming end of social solidarity. In that movie we perceive the sudden sadness, fog, and clouds descending over people's lives. The prison of Stammheim becomes a kind of metaphor for the everyday jail that social life was becoming in those years, in the passage from the restless decade after '68 to the decade of the neoliberal counter-revolution.

In Italy, the Red Brigades started their crazy, bloody campaigns. The riots in the streets of Rome, Bologna, and many other towns at the time were not peaceful meetings or friendly promenades. Violence became a central issue when the police reacted violently to the demonstrations, when the Government ordered their repression, and the police fatally shot students in Bologna, Rome, and elsewhere.

There was rage in the air. Not only because 15 percent of the population, especially young people, were unemployed. There was a kind of existential rage, a wave of insubordination, because the baby boomers all over the world were hit by the premonition that the welfare state was going to be dismantled, and that the modern horizon was starting to dissolve.

But 1977 was not only a time of unrest and insurrection. It is a turning point in the history of culture, technology and philosophical thought.

1977 is the year Steve Wozniak and Steve Jobs created the Apple trademark and, what is more, created the tools for spreading information technology. It is also the year Alain Minc and Simon Nora wrote *The Computerization of Society: A Report to the President of France*, a text that theorizes the coming dissolution of nation states due to the political effects of emerging telematics.

In that year, Yuri Andropov, secretary of the KGB, wrote a letter to Leonid Brezhnev, arguing that the Soviet Union was in danger of disappearing if the gap with the USA in the field of informatics was not bridged. It was the year that Jean François Lyotard wrote *The*

Postmodern Condition: A Report on Knowledge, in which he analyses the new organization of knowledge and the disappearance of the grand narrative of progressive modernity.

The year 1977 saw the last revolt of the communist proletarians of the twentieth century against capitalist rule and against the bourgeois state. But at the same time it saw the first revolt of the cognitariat, the intellectual workers, bearers of the *Technische Wissenschaft Intelligenz*.

In that year we can see the premonition of a new cultural process and a new social landscape. Italy had a special place in the cultural geography of that year. The tensions apparent everywhere in that country took the form of a strange movement, in which the concepts of political radicalism met the ideas of desire, rhizome, and schizopolitics, creating a new image and a new style of activism, focused on the politics of imagination.

What is special about the Italian movement of '77 is the fact that in its history you can see both faces of the changing times: the happy utopian side of creativity and the despair, hopelessness, and terror.

In the first part of that year, the colorful and utopian occupation of public space by the subversive crowds of "Metropolitan Indians" and "Mao-Dadaists" seemed to announce the possibility of collective happiness, a less workaholic society, and free access to the media. But after the explosion of the riots, after the killings and hundreds of arrests, the mood darkened, and a wave of despair surfaced, joining the punk sensibility, which originated in the London streets the same year.

The new generation of workers did not have much to do with the old tradition of the workers' parties. Nor did they have anything to do with the socialist ideology of a state-owned system. These young workers had much more to do with the hippy movement and the history of the art avant-garde. A massive refusal of the sadness of work was the leading element behind their protest.

What is the legacy of the movement of 1977?

The legacy and memory are ambiguous. We remember the cultural alertness and the feeling of shared happiness, and the freedom of daily life from the rules of work and money, but we also remember the dark side of the events, the fear and repression, and the dystopian content of the imagination. Today, at the end of the first decade of the new century, we are in a way witnessing the realization of that year's bad dream, the dystopian imagination coming true, nurtured by the movement and injected into the zeitgeist of the century's end.

In 1977, Ingmar Bergman produced the movie *The Serpent's Egg*, probably not one of his best, but a very disturbing insight into the construction of the totalitarian mind all the same. When I saw that film, right at the end of that year, I felt that something was directly speaking to me, to us. *The Serpent's Egg* is about the incubation of Nazism from 1923 to 1933. In those years, the egg of the serpent was slowly opening, giving birth to the monster. In the years following the students' uprising of March 1977, we felt something similar. We caught a whiff of a new totalitarianism in the making. A totalitarianism that was not founded on political power, but on the slow pervasion of the social mind.

Charlie Chaplin—the man who had recounted the dehumanization of the industrial process and shown the kindness of people who, despite being poor, were able to be human—passed away at the end of 1977, on the 25th of December. No more room for kindness in the postindustrial world of immaterial production. Then, in the final days of 1977, in the movie *Saturday Night Fever*, John Travolta portrayed the new hero of the working class, happy to be exploited all week long in exchange for some fun in the disco on Saturday night.

1977 was the year of mass youth suicide in Japan: the official figure being 784. What caused an outcry was the rapid succession, at the end of the summer holidays, of suicides by children: thirteen, to be exact, all amongst primary school children. What is disconcerting here isn't so much the number as the gratuitousness and the incomprehensibility of the gesture. In all these cases, there are no motivations or reasons for the acts. There is a striking lack of words, an inability on the part of the adults who lived with their children to predict, understand, or explain what happened.

In Japan as in Europe and the USA, 1977 is the year of passage beyond modernity. But whereas in Europe, this passage is signaled by the philosophy of authors such as Baudrillard, Virilio, Guattari, Deleuze, and by the political consciousness of mass movements such as the creative Italian autonomia or London punk, in North America it takes the form of a cultural explosion, a movement of urban transformations which is expressed in the artistic and musical "no wave"; in Japan, the passage already appears without mediation, as an inexplicable monstrosity which quickly becomes daily normality, the prevalent form of collective existence.

The collapse of the western mind has assumed a sneaking, sub-terranean, episodic trajectory since 1977, but on the threshold of the millennium, it takes on the precipitous rhythm of an uncontainable catastrophe. Consciousness of this trajectory perceives a danger in the accelerated pace of production, technology, and daily life, which Deleuze and Guattari call deterritorialization. Nowadays, the effects of that acceleration and deterritorialization are evident in the waves of fear, insecurity, and panic traversing the globalized social sphere.

Certain events have signaled this passage, becoming viruses, carrying information that reproduces itself, proliferating within and infecting the entire social organism. The exceptional event of the Twin Towers crashing in a cloud of dust following the deadly suicide of nineteen young Muslims is certainly the most impressive, the image-event that spectacularly inaugurates the new times. But the Columbine school massacre, which took place some years before, might have carried a more uncanny message, because it spoke of daily life, of American normality, the normality of a humanity that has lost all relation with what used to be human and that stumbles along looking for some impossible reassurance, searching for a substitute for emotions which it no longer knows.

CURSED BE THE PROPHET

I took part in the movements of the 1970s, and I was especially involved in the 1977 insurrections in Bologna and in Rome. Actually, that insurrection was less a political upheaval intended to change the form of political power, than an act of prediction, a collective prophecy aimed at engendering a social awareness, a consciousness that the world couldn't go on that way, that the profit economy was leading to devastation. I remember the insurgents of Bologna and Rome as a small crowd of crazy prophets, shaking their fists and crying enigmatic words in order to stop the march of the massive throng. We were not picturing the realities of those years so much as fighting against science fictional enemies. But those enemies (who we felt in our nightmares), came to life, afterwards, in the future of no future we are inhabiting now.

The vision of the future is cursed in many traditional cultures. In ancient times, the visionary who sees the future is tragic, and more tragic is the destiny of the prophet, who not only sees the future but reveals it to his contemporaries, who don't want to know. Tragic is the destiny of Cassandra and of Thyresia, because visions of the future should be the sole privilege of the gods. In the Christian world, the pious mind looks toward the origin, toward the time when god created everything. As we move away from that distant point, we lose sight of the light that was in the beginning. The future is the time of the Fall, of the dark getting deeper and deeper.

The modern mind reversed this perception, replacing the certainty of progress with the fear of the coming apocalypse. Since Bacon declared that knowledge is power, since the bourgeoisie bet on profits coming from investment, since history could be described as economic growth and civilization, the future has acquired a totally different meaning.

The future of the moderns had two reassuring qualities. First, it could be known, as the trends of human history could be traced in linear directions, and science could discover the laws of human evolution, which resembled the motion of the planets. Second, the future could be transformed by human will, by industry, economic technique, and political action. The emphasis on the future reaches its peak when economic science pretends to be able to foresee human action, its conflicts and choices. The twentieth century trusted in the future because it trusted in scientists who foretold it, and in policy makers able to make rational decisions.

But the century taught a bitter lesson to its utopians. At its end, the utopian imagination tended to turn dystopian: the nightmare of consciousness and science fiction were the central laboratories of this reversal. Once upon a time (in the days of Jules Verne or Isaac Asimov), science fiction was the elaboration of ever-expanding human dominance in space and in time. In the late century, SF imagination of the future vanished, became flat, narrow, and dark, and finally turned into a infinitely expanding present.

We have to run along the dynamic of disaster, said Robert Fripp in his 1979 *Frippertronics Manifesto*. In the 1980s, cyberpunk writers described the future as a never-ending dystopia. The prophet was once again cursed, as in ancient times.

We can see distant spaces, but distant time can no longer be seen. Space has expanded with no limits since we have entered virtual space. Virtual space is a vanishing point, the meeting point of infinite assemblages of enunciation.

Virtual time, on the contrary, does not exist. There is no such thing as a time of virtuality, because time is only in life, decomposition, and the becoming-death of the living. Virtuality is the collapse of the living; it is panic taking power in temporal perception.

This is why the future is no longer a comfortable subject. We understand that it's not likely to be known, just as we understand that the lines of intersection between the info-assemblages are so complex and fast that we cannot reduce them to any scientific law. And we are starting to doubt that the future can be governed by political strategies and military strength.

Every time political leaders of the world meet in those funny events called G8 or G20, the failure of political power—their lack of grasp on the future—becomes more evident. When they met in Sapporo, Hokkaido, in July 2008, and in L'Aquila in July 2009, the powerful men and women who lead the nations were supposed to make very important decisions about the crucial subject of climate change and its effects on the planetary ecosystem. But they were completely unable to say or do anything meaningful, so they have decided that, by 2050, toxic emissions will be reduced by half. How? Why? No answer. No political or technological action has been taken, no shorter deadline has been decided upon. Such a decision is like a shaman's ritual, like a rain dance. The complexity of the problem exceeds world politicians' powers of knowledge and influence. The future has escaped the grasp of political technique and everything has capsized, perhaps because of speed.

Absolute speed means the ubiquity of mind; not of the body, not of sensibility. Absolute speed is made possible by the network of signs. An all-pervading semiosis is secreted by innumerable interconnected brains. What are the effects on the social psychosphere? What is the acceleration going to produce in the field of erotic sensitivity, and in the very perception of others as embodied, as living organisms?

The future that the Futurists enthusiastically proclaimed is here at last, but it does not have the shape they imagined of an external metallic machine. It has arrived thanks to the potency of language, and the potency of the connection. It turns out that Italian Futurism had a grip on this possibility. Marinetti launched the cry: *Immaginazione senza fili*: WIRELESS IMAGINATION.

THE LAST UTOPIA

In the final decade of the century that trusted in the future, a new utopia takes form that can be labeled cyberculture—or Netculture or virtual culture, if you prefer. This utopia produces its own world in a much more efficient way than the previous century's utopias. The Net is the utopia of an infinite, virtual space where countless trajectories of billions of intelligent agents meet and create their economic, cultural, and psychic reality.

Etymologically speaking, Utopia is the place that does not exist. Similarly, Virtuality is a space that does not exist in the physical sense, although it can create effects of meaning, perception, and economic exchange. The Virtual Utopia, which spreads throughout the cultural imagination at the century's end, is doubly immaterial, that is, twice removed from the physical space of material life.

Of all the utopias of the twentieth century, the Virtual Utopia has produced the most consistent effects in the spheres of technology, economy, and daily life, giving way, in a sudden (but largely predicted) reversal, to the final dystopia: the disappearance of the human, or perhaps the submission of the human to the chain of technolinguistic automatisms.

The Net only exists in the shared mental space of its users, who are also its producers. This non-territory is the space of universal deterritorialization, in the parlance of Deleuze and Guattari. Every movement of deterritorialization causes a countereffect of reterritorialization. This is why, in the 1990s, the decade of the social construction of the Net, the globalization process grew alongside artificial revivals of nationalism and fundamentalism.

Building the Net implied a huge work of technical creation, engineering, and also a broad process of artistic creativity and philosophical innovation. In the sphere of cyberculture since the 1980s, different visions of the Net have been proposed, and contrasting philosophical imaginations have shaped the actual becoming of the Net.

The evolution of the Net cannot be reduced to a single definition, because it is an infinite space upon which it is futile to make final statements. Instead, different visions of the Net have coalesced and revealed different facets of the same process. These different visions function together because the Net is the place where different imaginations coevolve. A comprehensive phenomenology of Net Culture is beyond my intention and beyond my skills. Some scholars have written on this subject, I would especially mention Italian media theorist Carlo Formenti, for his *Trilogy of the Net* (*Incantati dalla Rete*, *Mercanti di futuro*, and *Cybersoviet*). Rather, I want just to point out the different perceptions of the future that have animated cyberculture since its birth.

The *Wired* imagination was, in my opinion, the most influential cultural stream of the 1990s. Since its start in 1993, *Wired* magazine, edited in San Francisco by Luis Rossetto, launched the idea that the Net would change the whole world of media, and became the general paradigm of technology and knowledge production. The Net is the concept, method, and trend.

Co-evolving with the World Wide Web and the first browsers for Net navigation, *Wired* addressed the inner circle of technonerds and cyberpunks. The huge achievement of the technophile, pro-market digerati of *Wired* Futurism was their understanding of a new economic trend based on the creation of virtual enterprises in the field of communication, finance, and personal services.

In this magazine, the libertarian soul merged with the market theology of neoliberal economists. The illusion of an infinite economic expansion in the field of virtual production nurtured the Utopia of the long boom and the ideology of the new economy. That illusion was powerful. The dotcom mania in the last years of the century created jobs, money, services, and goods, and helped to change the technological infrastructure of the global media system.

But at the same time, in a few hidden spaces of Net culture, some perceived the future in darker tones. Canadian theorist Arthur Kroker, for instance, may be labeled as the harbinger of the dystopian vision of the Net. In 1994, Kroker and Weinstein published the book *Data Trash*, a remarkable insight into the psychosocial effects of technochange. He forecasts the creation of a cyberauthoritarianism, based on the massification and simplification of the Web. As he wrote:

> The information highway is the antithesis of the Net, in much the same way as the virtual class must destroy the *public dimension* of the Internet for its own survival.... for the virtual class, content slows the speed of virtualized exchange, and meaning becomes the antagonistic contradiction of data.... Data is the antivirus of meaning—telematic information refuses to be slowed

down by the drag-weight of content. And the virtual class seeks to exterminate the *social* possibilities of the Internet. (Kroker and Weinstein 1994, 7–8).

Kroker and Weinstein are concerned about the removal of the body in virtual space, and foresee a violent comeback of the body, in the aggressive form of Retro-Fascism. Kroker's thought develops some of Baudrillard's ideas in the direction of a theory of the virtual class. The virtual class is a class that does not actually exist. It is only the abstraction of the fractal ocean of productive micro-actions of cognitive workers. Virtual class is a useful concept, but it does not comprehend the social and bodily existence of those people who perform virtual tasks. The social existence of virtual workers is not virtual, the sensual body of the virtual worker is not virtual. This is why from the theory of the virtual class we have to extrapolate a theory of the cognitariat, or cognitive proletariat, in order to emphasize the physical (erotic, social, neurological) side of the desires and diseases of the workers involved in the net economy.

Semiocapital puts neuropsychical energies to work, and submits them to the speed of electronic machinery. It compels our cognition, our emotional hardware to follow the rhythm of net-productivity. Cyberspace overloads cybertime, because cyberspace is an unbounded sphere, whose speed can accelerate without limits. But cybertime (the time of attention, memory, and imagination) cannot speed beyond a limit. If it does, it cracks. And it is actually cracking, collapsing under the stress of hyperproductivity. An epidemic of panic is spreading throughout the circuits of the social brain. An epidemic of depression is following the outbreak of panic. The crisis of the new economy at the beginning of the zero zero decade has to be seen as consequence of this nervous breakdown.

Once upon a time, Marx spoke about overproduction, meaning the excess of available goods that couldn't be absorbed by the social market. In the sphere of net-production, it is the social brain that is assaulted by an overwhelming supply of attention-demanding goods. This is why the social factory has become the factory of unhappiness: the assembly line of net-production is directly exploiting the emotional energy of the virtual class. We have to become aware of it; we have to recognize ourselves as cognitarians. Flesh, body, desire, in permanent electrostimulation.

Biologist, philosopher, and journalist at the same time, Kevin Kelly was the animator of *CoEvolution Quarterly* in the 1980s, then editor of *Wired* magazine for many years. In his book *Out of Control*, he speaks of a bio-informatic superorganism that is the result of the synergy of countless human minds, and is placed outside of the reach of human control, understanding, and government:

> As very large webs penetrate the world, we see the first glimpses of what emerges from that net—machines that become alive, smart, and evolve—a neobiological civilization. There is a sense in which a global mind also emerges in the network culture. The global mind is a union of computer and nature, of telephones and human brains and more. It is a very large complexity of in-determinate shape governed by an invisible hand of its own. We humans will be unconscious of what the global mind ponders. This is not because we are not smart enough, but because the de-sign of a mind does not allow the part to understand the whole. The particular thoughts of the global mind, and its subsequent actions, will be out of our control and beyond our understand-ing. (Kelly 1994, 260)

Utopia and dystopia mix in Kelly's vision. No subglobal mind will be able to understand the superior design of the global mind, because its complexity is unattainable for the individual brain: instead, Kelly speaks of hive mind.

No subglobal entity (a party, a government, a group of decision makers) will be able to change the course of events, because the course of events is determined by the integrated work of a global mind mas-tered by no one. Human behavior tends more and more to resemble the behavior of a swarm. The swarm may be similar to a group of people who run toward a train station in order to catch the last train before it's too late. But a crowd is more aleatory and unpredictable than a swarm.

The behavior of persons who take part in a network cannot be aleatory, because participation in a network presupposes and com-mands compliance with the rules. The principle governing the swarm is internalization: living organisms follow psychical and behavioral au-tomatisms because this is their way of relating to the environment. The components of a swarm are not conscious, or are not fully conscious that their behaviors are driven by inbuilt automatism.

Joining the legacy of the liberal thought of Adam Smith, and legitimizing the neoliberal trend that was triumphant in the 1990s, Kelly (1994, 33) speaks of an invisible hand that is almost heavenly, happily leading to an end of real-life suffering and conflicts on the planet. He writes: "Hidden in the Net is the mystery of the Invisible Hand—control without authority." In the network, as in the swarm, participants must comply with the rules embedded in the program if they want to continue to participate in the game. The connection demands operational compliance, not any reciprocal comprehension on the level of meaning, or affection.

Connection is interoperability and it makes possible the circulation of abstract information. It involves conscious and sensitive bodies, but the conscious and sensitive body is only a passive carrier of connection. Consciousness is only an operational ability to react. And sensitivity is slowness, hindering acceleration and competition.

Kelly is postulating the intrinsic rationality of the global mind, following the Smithian and liberal myth of the Invisible Hand. In the digital age, the invisible hand is the system of technological, cognitive, and economic automatisms. In the recombinant technosphere, the investments, the dislocations of capital, and the economic balance of states no longer depend on the choices of policy makers, or on political strategies—they depend more and more on the network of automated steps of a program embedded in the social machine. This program of programs is acquiring the strength and inescapability of natural necessity.

The process of decision making and projecting a future in which one future among many can be selected depends less and less on human will. We may call it the paradox of the decider: as the circulation of information becomes faster and more complex, the time available for the elaboration of relevant information becomes shorter. The more space taken by the available information, the less time there is for understanding and conscious choice. This is why the interdependence between data and decisions is more and more embedded in infomachinery, in technolinguistic interfaces. This is why the execution of the program is entrusted to automated procedures that human operators can neither change nor ignore.

The machine pretends to be neutral, purely mathematical, but we know that its procedures are only the technical reification of social interests: profit, accumulation, competition—these are the criteria underlying the automatic procedures embedded in the machine. Human volition is reduced to a procedural pretense.

Virtual Utopia has eaten the future, removing it to the sphere of imagination and willpower. Virtual Utopia culminates in the dystopian totalitarianism of the Logic of Necessity.

In the year 2000, *Wired* magazine published a text by Bill Joy titled "Why the Future Does Not Need Us." This text harshly conflicts with the spirit of the magazine, and is an impressive monument to the dystopian consciousness of someone who isn't a radical philosopher, but a man of science and technology. The starting point of Joy's thought is quite similar to the core of Kelly's, but Joy subverts Kelly's Futurist enthusiasm. Focusing on the coming developments of nanotechnology, Joy, like Kelly, depicts the trend toward the creation of a global mind embedded in the logical, linguistic, operational technosphere. If Kelly invites us to unquestioningly welcome the trend without demanding control of the global mind's infinite complexity, Joy's tone is overpowered by anxiety, by the fear of creating, like doctor Frankenstein, a dystopian monster from whom we'll never escape. Referring to the proliferation of intelligent nanomachines and the interweaving of information technologies, biotechnologies, and simulation processes, he describes a possible scenario in which human beings will be obsolete, irrelevant, because decisions are more and more in the hands (in the brains) of intelligent machines.

This is perhaps an old humanism, with its gloomy imagination bequeathed by Orwell, Bradbury, and Ballard. Regardless, in the first decade of the new millennium these imaginations have woven the fabric of social life.

INVERSION OF THE FUTURE

The future has reversed its polarity, caution Miguel Benasayag and Gérard Schmidt (2007) in *Les passions tristes* [*The Age of Sad Passions*], in which they reflect on their long therapeutic practice with youth in the *banlieues* of Paris. In the modern era, the future was imagined thanks to metaphors of progress. Scientific research and economical entrepreneurship in the centuries of modern development were inspired by the idea that knowledge will lead to an ever more complete mastery of the human universe. The Enlightenment sanctions this conception, and positivism makes it an absolute belief. Marxist revolutionary ideologies, guided by an historicist and dialectical vision, also imagine the future on the basis of a progressive, teleological model. The present contains, in the form of contradiction, a potential that history is necessarily destined to resolve. It is from the dialectical solution of present contradictions that a social form free from poverty and war will be born. This form is what the Marxist movement calls communism. In the last part of the twentieth century these philosophical premises disintegrated. But what has disappeared, more than anything else, is the credibility of a progressive model for the future.

> The future, the very idea of the future, now bears an opposite sign. Pure positivity becomes negativity, and the promise becomes a threat. Of course, knowledge has developed, but it is unable to suppress human suffering and it feeds the pervading sadness and pessimism. (Benasayag and Schmidt 2007, 29)

The future becomes a threat when the collective imagination becomes incapable of seeing alternatives to trends leading to devastation, increased poverty, and violence. This is precisely our current situation, because capitalism has become a system of techno-economic automatisms that politics cannot evade. The paralysis of the will (the impossibility of politics) is the historical context of today's depression epidemic.

The morning of April 20, 2007, I was reading the Italian newspaper *Il Corriere della Sera*. On the upper corner of page 20, there was a report about the exploits of Cho Seung Hui, the Korean boy who went to look for his girlfriend at Virginia Tech and, not finding her, shot about thirty students and professors at the school.

Weapons, Death, Delirium
The Killer's Video on TV

That was the title of the article: in the picture next to it we see the boy holding two guns, arms spread apart like an advertisement for the Lara Croft video games.

Up to now, nothing unusual. Every newspaper on the planet was talking about Cho Seung Hui that day. After killing two people at eight-thirty, and before coming back to Virginia Tech to kill many more, he had gone home, prepared a video-testament, and sent it to the NBC network which, of course, decided to air it.

But what really got my attention was the image at the bottom of page 20. At first, after quickly glancing at it, I thought it was part of the same story. Against a black background, I saw the image of a woman with Asiatic, actually Korean, features. She was wearing dark sunglasses, which gave her a stark, aggressive, proud look, and she was portrayed in three different and overlapping poses. In the middle, she is represented frontally, rotating her torso, projecting her head forward and her left arm backward, as if launching a projectile right at you.

On the right, the same person is raising one leg and lifting a brief-case made of white synthetic fabric just like her suit. On the left, the position becomes decidedly violent: we see the woman violently kicking an invisible target with her left leg, while her folded right arm seems to be collecting all her available strength. It was an advertisement for Intel Corporation, promoting the new Intel Core 2 Duo processor. In fact, in the same image, you can read a slogan proclaiming:

INCREASE YOUR FREEDOM
Multiply your performance with the Intel Core 2 processor

Why did they choose a woman for those poses? The Far East trans-mits aggressive vibrations, an indefatigable work ethic, activity, per-manent personal mobilization, success in international competitions.

Cho and the advertising team at Intel share the same imaginary of reference. The message coming out of the young man's recorded images is the same as the one communicated by the advertisers.

Deadly suicidal explosions are often associated with a pathologi-cal diagnosis of depression. Many have denounced the violent suicidal and/or homicidal effects in patients treated with antidepressants that, rather than dealing with the deep psychological implications of depres-sion, simply remove the inhibition to act.

Depression cannot explain Cho's explosion of violence. Cho's act is complex, creatively conceived and articulated. It is a work of art sat-urated with symbolic referents taken from contemporary terror-pop.

Against a depressive background, confirmed also by the text written by Cho, we see emerging a powerful reaction, aided by easily available substances: psychotropic drugs, terror-pop imagery, precise and powerful weapons. I don't know what kind of substances Cho might have been taking.

The *Corriere della Sera* suggests, by the casual nature of its advertisements, an interpretive key that can't be reduced to a diagnosis of depression: Cho's violent act is tied to a saturation of emotional circuits, a short circuit caused by overload. This explosively violent behavior follows the loss of control of the relation between informational stimuli and emotional elaboration.

This murderous *acting out* can be the consequence of a depression treated with anti-inhibitory drugs that have no effect on the cause of depression.

A whole semiotic universe has grafted itself onto this pharmacological disinhibition, a cascade of semiostimuli that brought the organism to an uncontrollable hyperexcitation.

The object of study is the panic-depressive cycle. The message of the Intel corporation, like the whole flux of advertising stimuli, mobilizes a competitive aggression, the violent transgression of rules, the impulsive affirmation of one's own expressivity. The *multitasking* staged by Intel is the most powerful factor in the intensification of productivity typical of cognitive labor. But multitasking also destructures our faculty for processing information rationally, and it overexcites our emotional system in a pathological manner. In the newspeak of semiocapitalist hyperneoliberalism the expression "Multiply your freedom" actually means "Multiply your productivity." It should be no surprise that the exposure to the informational-advertising-productive stimulating flux produces panic-like, neurasthenic effects and a pathological irritability. But the succession from mobilizing stimulation of nervous energy to violent action isn't linear, because, if that were the case, all workers undergoing an intense nervous exploitation would become murderers, and this is still not happening. The circuit is more complicated than that. The constant mobilization of nervous energies can lead to a depressive reaction: the frustration of our attempts to act and compete leads the subject to withdraw his or her libidinal energy from the social arena. Our frustrated narcissism retreats and the energy just shuts itself off.

Therapeutic action, at this point, does not address the deep cause of depression, because, as we shall see, this cause cannot be attacked by a pharmacological therapy. The therapeutic treatment of depression implies a long and deep process of linguistic elaboration, while a pharmacological treatment can act effectively only on the inhibiting blockages, not on the mental causes of depression. And this unblocking action can stimulate a violent action characterized by a depressive background.

Intensification of nervous stimuli, retreat of libidinal investment, painful understanding of narcissism: these are the main aspects of a very widely spread pathological profile in today's society. We can clearly distinguish the pathologies caused by overload (panic, attention disorders, dyslexia) from the ones caused by disinvestment (depression and even autism). But this conceptual distinction should be followed by the recognition that these pathologies, whose origins are different, act simultaneously and complementarily, causing extremely violent manifestations.

Of course, the drugs that remove the inhibitions to act without touching on the depressive core can end up unleashing reckless acts, pure and simple explosions of self-destructive or violent forces:

> After 1980, anxiety neuroses have been divided in two categories: the panic attack and general anxiety syndrome. These two pathologies have quickly migrated in the depressive field, because they can be better treated by antidepressants than with anxiety-reducing medications. Today, anxiety is part of the depressive field. (Ehrenberg 1998, 25)

The basic pathogenic picture emerging from the era of the first connective generation is characterized by the hypermobilizing of nervous energies, by informational overload, by a constant straining of our attention faculties. A particular aspect and an important consequence of this nervous hypermobilization is the rarity of bodily contact, the physical and psychical solitude of the infospheric individual. Within this condition, we have to study depression as a secondary epidemic phenomenon, perfectly integrated in the psychotic-panic framework of the first connective generation.

Conceptually, I find it interesting to distinguish between anxiety and depressive syndromes, because in the first I see the effect of a stimulus overload, while the second are caused by a disinvestment of energy. But if we want to explain the epidemic explosion of violence at the dawn of our new millennium, we have to recognize their connection. A frustrated hyperexcitement leads to a disinvestment of libidinal energy that we call depression. But the subject can explode the depressive block with psychotropic drugs or potentially deadly schocks to behavior.

Depression can't be reduced to the psychological field. It questions the very foundation of being.

Melancholic depression can be understood in relation to the circulation of sense. Faced with the abyss of nonsense, friends talk to friends, and together they build a bridge across the abyss. Depression questions the reliability of this bridge. Depression doesn't see the bridge. It's not on its radar. Or maybe it sees that the bridge does not exist. Depression doesn't trust friendship, or doesn't recognize it. This is why it cannot perceive sense, because there is no sense that isn't made in shared spaces.

Sense is the projection of an intellectual and emotional investment. We can say that sense is the effect of a libidinal investment in interpretation, in the construction of meaning.

The last book by Gilles Deleuze and Félix Guattari, *What Is Philosophy?*, contains reflections on old age, friendship, chaos, and speed. The theme of depression (always repressed or even denied elsewhere in their work) finally emerges.

> Chaos is defined not so much by its disorder as by the infinite speed with which every form taking shape in it vanishes. It is a void that is not a nothingness but a *virtual*, containing all possible particles and drawing out all possible forms, which spring up only to disappear immediately, without consistency or reference, without consequence. Chaos is an infinite speed of birth and disappearance. (Deleuze and Guattari 1994, 118)

And they add:

> Nothing is more distressing than a thought that escapes itself, than ideas that fly off, that disappear hardly formed, already eroded by forgetfulness or precipitated into others that we no longer master. These are infinite *variabilities*, the appearing

and disappearing of which coincide. They are infinite speeds that blend into the immobility of the colorless… (Deleuze and Guattari 1994, 201)

The infinite acceleration of the world with respect to the mind is the feeling of being definitively cut off from the sense of the world. Sense isn't found in the world, but in what we are able to create. What circulates in the sphere of friendship, of love, of social solidarity is what allows us to find sense. Depression can be defined as a lack of sense, as an inability to find sense through action, through communication, through life. The inability to find sense is first of all the inability to create it.

Let's think about depression caused by love. The lover structures the creation of sense around the person who is the object of his or her desire. The object of love is the magnet attracting the desiring energy. If this object disappears, the ability to create sense is annihilated and, consequently, nothing makes sense anymore. "Nothing makes sense for me," says the abandoned lover, and this sentence has a very concrete, not a metaphoric, meaning. Julia Kristeva, in *Black Sun*, writes:

> The depressive mood constitutes itself as a narcissistic support, negative to be sure, but nevertheless presenting the self with an integrity, nonverbal though it might be. Because of that, the depressive affect makes up for symbolic invalidation and interruption (the depressive's "that's meaningless") and at the same time protects it against proceeding to the suicidal act. That protection, however, is a flimsy one. The depressive denial that destroys the meaning of the symbolic also destroys the act's meaning and leads the subject to commit suicide without anguish of disintegration, as a reuniting with archaic nonintegration, as lethal as it is jubilatory, "oceanic" (Kristeva 1992, 19)

If we consider depression the suspension of the sharing of time, as an awakening to a senseless world, then we have to admit that, philosophically speaking, depression is simply the moment that comes closest to truth.

The depressed subject doesn't at all lose the faculty to rationally elaborate the content of his life and his knowledge: on the contrary, his or her vision can reach an absolute radicality of understanding.

Depression allows us to see what we normally hide from ourselves through the continuous circulation of a reassuring collective narrative. Depression sees what public discourse hides. Depression is the best condition from which to access the void that is the ultimate truth.

At the same time, though, depression paralyzes any ability to act, to communicate, to share. It's precisely on this inability to act, which is psychically secondary and pragmatically decisive, that antidepressants have their effect.

I don't intend to deny that drugs can be effective in treating the symptoms of depression, nor even that, by removing the symptoms, we can put back into motion a temporarily paralyzed energy, thereby overcoming the very core of the depression. But I want to emphasize the fact that depression is different from its symptoms, and that the cure for depression is the revitalization of singularity, and the conscious acceptance of its impermanence or finitude.

In *La Fatigue d'être soi*, Alain Ehrenberg starts from the idea that depression is a disturbance that must be understood within a social context. In today's highly competitive environment, the depressive syndrome produces an infernal spiral. Depression is caused by a wound to our narcissistic tendencies, and this wound reduces the libidinal energy that we invest in our actions. Consequently, depression is reinforced because it produces a diminution in our activity level and in our ability to compete.

> Depression triumphs when the disciplinary model of behavioral management, the rules concerning authority and conformity typical of a time when interdictions assigned their destiny to the different social classes, has retreated in favor of norms that encourage everyone to individual achievement, ordering people to become themselves. The consequence of this new normativity is that the entire responsibility of our lives is located not only in ourselves, but also in the collective space. Depression is an illness of responsibility, dominated by a feeling of inadequacy. The depressed subject is not capable, he is tired of being him or herself. (Ehrenberg 1998, 10)

It's not surprising that depression is spreading at a time when an entrepreneurial and competitive ideology is becoming dominant. Since the early 1980s, after the defeat of the working-class movements and the affirmation of neoliberal ideology, the idea that we should all be entrepreneurs has gained social recognition. Nobody can conceive his or her life in a more relaxed and egalitarian manner. S/he who relaxes may very well end up in the streets, in the poorhouse, or in jail.

The so-called neoliberal reforms that are continuously imposed on an increasingly fragmented, defeated, impotent society, which has been crushed by the dominant ideologies, are directed toward the destruction of any economic security for working people, and to expose every worker's life to the risks of the entrepreneurial profession. In the past, risk was the job of the capitalist, who invested in his or her own abilities, obtaining enormous gains or suffering painful failures. But economic risk was his business. Other people ranged from misery to relative prosperity, but they were not encouraged to take risks in order to have more. But today "we are all capitalist," as the ideologues of neoliberal reform loudly proclaim, and therefore we all have to take risks. Pensions will no longer be given in exchange for the savings accumulated thanks to a life of work, but they have to be tied to pension funds that will either produce fabulous revenues or fail miserably, leaving us destitute in our old age. The essential idea is that we all should consider life as an economic venture, as a race where there are winners and losers.

Ehrenberg's analysis sketches the genealogy of the depressive pathologies typical of a generalized entrepreneurial society. The published version of Foucault's 1978–9 seminar, *The Birth of Biopolitics*, also identifies the spread of the free enterprise economic model in our ways of living and thinking as the decisive trait of our age. It is the age of neoliberal totalitarianism.

> In corporate life, the disciplinary models typical of Fordism are retreating in favor of norms that push employees to adopt autonomous behaviors. Participatory management, expression groups, quality circles constitute new ways of enforcing authority, aimed at impressing a spirit of obedience in every salaried worker. These ways of regulating and dominating the work force are founded on initiative more than on mechanical obedience. A sense of responsibility, the ability to evolve and to create projects, motivation, flexibility: these qualities delineate a new managerial

liturgy. The issue is the mobilization of affects and mental capacities much more than dressing the bodies of the salaried workers. The obligations and the ways of defining the problem change: from the mid-1980s on, both occupational medicine and entrepreneurial sociological research emphasize the new prevalence of anxiety, psychosomatic disorders, and depression. Corporate life is the antechamber of depression. (Ehrenberg 1998, 199).

In the 1990s, a new pharmacological fashion explodes: substances such as sertraline (Zoloft) and fluorexine (Prozac) flood the market. Unlike benzodiazepines, a family of drugs that includes diazepam (Valium) and bromazepam (Lexotan), these new products don't have a hypnotic, relaxing, and anxiety-reducing effect; rather, they have a euphoric effect and allow the unblocking of the inhibition to act that constitutes one of the behavioral manifestations of depression.

In the mid-1990s, the decade that gave the biggest push to the cognitive economy, and that needed the total mobilization of creative labor's mental energies, a true mythology of Prozac was born. That product became (and still is) a bestseller in pharmacies around the world. The entire managerial class of the global economy went into a constant state of euphoria and psychic alteration. The economic decisions of the global managerial class are a faithful reflection of the substance that allowed "deciders" to see only the euphoric aspect of the world, while stubbornly ignoring the devastating effects of economic euphoria. For years, decisions have been made with Zoloft-impregnated brains or after having swallowed millions of Prozac tablets. At a certain point, after the financial crisis of the spring 2000 and the political crisis of September 11, 2001, the world managerial class went into a depressive phase. To cure its own internal void, or maybe to remove the depressing truth of its ethical defeat, the world managerial class has injected itself with a new, dangerous substance: War, an amphetamine that serves to reinvest an aggressivity now destined to destroy the residual energies of the human species and the planet.

In recent decades, the organism has been exposed to an increasing mass of neuromobilizing stimuli. The acceleration and intensification of nervous stimuli on the conscious organism seems to have thinned the cognitive membrane that we might call sensibility. The conscious organism needs to accelerate its cognitive, gestural, kinetic reactivity.

The time available for responding to nervous stimuli has been dramatically reduced. This is perhaps why we seem to be seeing a reduction of the capacity for empathy. Symbolic exchange among human beings is elaborated without empathy, because it becomes increasingly difficult to perceive the existence of the body of the other in time. In order to experience the other as a sensorial body, you need time, time to caress and smell. The time for empathy is lacking, because stimulation has become too intense. Can we hypothesize a direct relationship between the expansion of the infosphere (acceleration of stimuli and nervous solicitation, of the rhythms of cognitive response) and the crumbling of the sensory membrane that allows human beings to understand that which cannot be verbalized, that which cannot be reduced to codified signs?

Reducers of complexity such as money, information, stereotypes, or digital network interfaces have simplified the relationship with the other, but when the other appears in flesh and blood, we cannot tolerate its presence, because it hurts our (in)sensibility. The video-electronic generation does not tolerate armpit or pubic hair. One needs perfect compatibility in order to interface corporeal surfaces in connection. Smooth generation. Conjunction finds its ways through hairs and the imperfections of exchange. It is capable of analogical reading, and heterogeneous bodies can understand each other even if they don't have an interfacing language.

chapter two

THE

ZERO

ZERO

DECADE

THE SECOND PART

of this book is focused on the social and political landscape of the first decade of the new millennium, particularly on the changing perception of the future, the erosion of the very foundations of the social civilization that implemented the ideology of progress.

The style of these texts is varied, because here I have collected texts written over this decade and published in different contexts. I've rewritten parts here and there, but the reader should not expect a coherent development—rather, scattered insights and overviews of a multiform and changing landscape. The first text is dedicated to the present situation, following the failure of the 2009 UN Climate Change Conference in Copenhagen, "COP15."

FROM SEATTLE TO COPENHAGEN

"Copenhagen, which had been co-branded for the talks on billboards with Coke and Siemens as Hopenhagen, was looking more like Nopenhagen." So writes Amy Goodman (n.d.), commenting on the failure of the 2009 climate summit held in Denmark. Ten years after the Seattle riots, while the world political system seems unable to take any action for the governance of the global environment, the movement is searching for a way out from the disaster that decades of neoliberal policy have prepared. The prospect of a double disruption—environmental and social—of the very foundations of modern civilization is more and more possible, but the ruling class is reaffirming the strategy that generated the present situation, based on dogmas of competition, profit, and growth:

> There is a crisis of belief in the future, leaving us with the prospect of an endless, deteriorating present that hangs around by sheer inertia. In spite of all this turmoil—this time of "crisis" when it seems like everything could, and should, have changed—it paradoxically feels as though history has stopped. There is an unwillingness, or inability, to face up to the scale of the crisis. Individuals, companies and governments have hunkered down,

hoping to ride out the storm until the old world re-emerges in a couple of years. Attempts to wish the "green shoots" of recovery into existence mistake an epochal crisis for a cyclical one; they are little more than wide-eyed boosterism. Yes, astronomical sums of money have prevented the complete collapse of the financial system, but the bailouts have been used to prevent change, not initiate it. We are trapped in a state of limbo. (Turbulence 2009, 3)

The ideological bases of neoliberalism have been shaken by the financial crisis and by the ecological awareness fostered by climate change.

In its heyday, neoliberal ideology was effective in banishing all other thought because it posed as nonideological, as merely the "reasonable" application of the "science" of utility. Today, however, it is possible to see (and say) that the presuppositions of these reasonable decisions were, of course, ideological. The market *does not* tend toward equilibrium, the maximization of self-interest *can* override instincts of self-preservation and lead to suboptimal outcomes, and in times of crisis any trickle down *is* reverted into the upstream splurge of bailouts. The premises of those supposedly nonideological arguments—such as the transformation of "the market" into a natural given governed by scientific laws available to *ortho-dox* ("correct opinion") but not to *hetero-dox* ("other opinion") economists—have now been debunked. Hardcore neoliberal ideology will cease to shape the space of politics by defining its terms, what is good and bad (*investment* rather than public *spending, efficient* private versus *inefficient* public, *markets* not *planning*), and pulling the center of gravity of the debate toward itself. Neoliberal orthodoxy no longer forms the middle ground of politics in regard to which all other opinions have to position themselves. (ibid., 4).

Nevertheless, the dogmas of economic fanaticism are imposing their rule. *Newsweek* titled its 2010 special edition: *Is that all?*, meaning that the promise of a deep change after the financial collapse had been disregarded. The old bourgeoisie had been able to reconcile business interests with the civil progress of society. It was a territorialized class, whose wealth depended on physical goods and common infrastructures. The deterritorialized financial class has no interest in long-term social survival. The global job market has destroyed the bargaining power of workers, and global wages are steadily falling everywhere. The social order founded on the power of workers has been eroded by neoliberal deregulation, and is now showing signs of collapse.

In this context, COP15 took place in December 2009. The central subject of the summit was not really the environment. It was the debt that western imperialism has incurred with the planet and humankind: the debt of colonization and genocide, of systematic exploitation and environmental ravage. For the western population today, the most urgent things are saving the habitability of the environment and avoiding the collapse of the physical conditions that made civilization possible. For the poor of the global South (and also for the poor of the northern metropolis), the prospect is different, as they never experienced the same advantages of modern civilization.

After financial collapse and American military defeat, the West seems to have lost its ability to blackmail, and the world is asking for reparations. The western nations are no longer able to impose their agenda on the newly industrialized countries and the dispossessed of the planet. The West feels urgency of the climatic change and is finally aware of the dangerous effects of pollution in general. But the West has created the problem, and has founded its wealth on the devastation of the common environment. The dispossessed don't fear climatic hell the way the western population does, because the dispossessed are already living in hell. So what is coming out from the Copenhagen summit is this frightening scenario: the global South is using climatic change as a weapon against the global North. If you don't want to drown, you have to pay the debt accumulated during five centuries. Will the West be able to meet the challenge, or will the confrontation lead to further disruption of the geopolitical balance and new wars?

Evo Morales said at COP15:

> To pay this debt, [the industrialized countries] should reduce their emissions and absorb their greenhouse gases in a way that there exists a fair distribution of atmospheric space between all of the countries, taking into consideration their population, because the countries that are on the path of development need atmospheric space for their development.

The third component of climate debt is the paying of reparations, reparations for damages that have been created by the irrationally industrialized countries. For humanity together, it's shameful that the western countries have only offered $10 billion for climate change. I was looking at some figures. The United States—how much does the United States spend to export terrorism to Afghanistan, to export terrorism to Iraq, and to export military bases to South America? They don't only spend millions, but billions and trillions.[1]

The concept of "debt" implies a bet on the future: debt is the handover of a part of our future in exchange for something that we are consuming now. The concept of "guilt" also implies the idea that we are taking something now that we'll have to atone for in the future (maybe in the afterworld). Not surprisingly, in Aramaic (Jesus's language), debt and guilt are the same word. In the Judeo-Christian cultural sphere, guilt founds human relations and historical time. Atonement is the future that awaits the sinner. If you are able to atone for your guilt in this life, you'll be among the elected by God; if you persevere in your guilty behavior, you'll pay with eternal punishment.

In the Judeo-Christian world, debt and guilt are similar, so one can expect that if you take something today, you will give it back tomorrow, if you don't want to die in mortal sin. Once the principle of restitution is agreed upon in the economic sphere, credit becomes possible as a system of borrowing on the future. The dynamic of capitalist accumulation is based on this perpetual process of investment in a borrowed future, and the very idea of future becomes a common cultural dimension when capitalism grants the relationship between present borrowing and future repayment. But if the promise of restitution fails, if those who take part in the game of guilt and atonement, of debt and restitution, lose faith in the future, then what? If those who borrow know that the world is going to end soon, or simply don't care about the other's future, what happens?

In *The Transparency of Evil*, Baudrillard (1993b) speaks of the orbitalization of debt. At a certain point of capitalist history, Baudrillard writes, debt started to grow vertiginously, so as to become purely virtual

---

1   www.democracynow.org/2009/12/16/bolivian_president_
evo_morales_shameful_for

and abandon the sphere of terrestrial relationships, like a satellite orbiting the Earth. Circulating from one bank to the next, from one country to the next, debt has taken off, like space debris. Baudrillard argues that if those billions and trillions would fall back to Earth, it would be a true catastrophe.

What has happened since September 2008 is exactly what Baudrillard ruled out as an impossible event. Trillions of dollars floating in orbit have fallen down to Earth, and virtual finance has provoked a collapse of the economy and, it seems, is also going to provoke a collapse of the world's environment. Baudrillard himself, in the last years of his life, began to think about the possibility of a return from the virtual to the material sphere. Debt has allowed a constant increase in consumption by the bulimic population of the rich world. But the physical planet is now besieged by sickness, waste, and drought.

If the debt is now unrecoverable, if the West is unable to repay it, I think that an age of violence and misery is going to follow.

The only way to pay *this* debt is to change the very idea of future as growth.

ON THE BRINK OF DISASTER

Since the early 1980s, the world has been governed by an elite that has invested all of the social energies at its disposal in the economy of profit. From Reagan's America to Deng Xiaoping's China, "get rich" became the watchword, the only imperative. On this criterion a ruling class was selected, with no culture other than that of profit, no values other than those of robbery, no strategy other than that of domination and submission. In the name of the interests of the profit economy, it was seen as legitimate to destroy all social defenses, all rights, all forms of life and culture.

Recombinant technologies (computer and biotechnologies) have been used as instruments of economic profit maximization. The profit economy has deeply permeated the epistemic structures and applications of these technologies, which contain an unprecedented capacity to mould and mutate the human genetic make-up (at the physical, psychic, and cognitive level). A real mutation began to modify the collective body in accordance with a paradigm dominated by the criterion of economic profit.

A few big institutions of world governance, which nobody ever elected, have guided the globalization process that Web technologies have frenetically accelerated. These institutions (IMF, WTO, World Bank, etc.) have imposed the interests of large global enterprises on the economic, social, political, technological, and cultural development of each country of the world. This reduced social defenses against the intrusiveness of profit, and led to the privatization of socially indispensable services and the decline in public spending on health and education. The end result, largely visible today, is an increase in ignorance, a diffusion of aggressiveness, and devastation of the environment.

During the 1990s, the development of the economy was prodigious, not only in western countries. Globalization gave birth to new productive classes in eastern countries and enormously expanded the purchasing power of the western minority integrated into the profit economy. New productive sectors (primarily, those linked to the digitalization of production and communication) sustained demand for the entire decade and determined the formation of a mass capitalism to which a conspicuous part of the western population participated, through a huge diffusion of the social entrepreneurial function and a progressive identification of labor and capital, especially in the high tech sectors. Cognitive labor became the leading sector of global production, shaped by the economy-driven ideology and identified with the entrepreneurial function, participating at the forefront of mass financial capitalism (dotcom mania). In the meantime, the length of the work day, which had been in decline up until the end of the 1970s, began to increase again after the world victory of neoliberalism. The free time gained through a century of workers' struggle was progressively subsumed to the rule of profit and transformed into fragmented and diffused labor. Social energies were progressively subsumed to economic competition. Those who didn't run got run over. Society started running frantically and many broke down.

The competitive mobilization of social energies rapidly brought about the breakdown of the social organism; this was simultaneously nervous and economic (but the economy had already become a mental sphere). From the spring of 2000, the expansive cycle of the economy started breaking down, as a result of various trends:

a) the demand for new technologies progressively fell; the fall of profit in innovative sectors accelerated precipitously;

b) the prospect of an exhaustion of nonrenewable energy sources caused ferocious competition;

c) a crisis of overproduction spread into innovative sectors. Huge quantities of semiocommodities remained unsold. This provoked a fall in the stock markets, followed by a crisis of trust in the future of mass capitalism;

d) the investment of psychic energies into the competitive race provoked a saturation of attention, to the point of creating the conditions for a generalized breakdown.

Some global corporations entered a crisis. It became apparent that the ruling groups of the new capitalism had violated all the rules of economic correctness, robbed collective resources, and governed production without strategic competence. Their attention had been entirely focused on the achievement of maximum immediate profit. Faith in the ruling group of the world economy crumbled. Mass capitalism began to fall. Unemployment started rising, especially amongst the generation that was now entering the labor market, who had grown up with a belief in the eternal continuity of economic development.

In the meantime, a new political class, one that got rich through robbery and achieved consensus through its full control over the media system and the growth of ignorance, came to govern different western countries. For twenty years, the collective brain had been bombarded by symbols of consumerism and competitive and aggressive violence. A sort of lumpen-bourgeoisie was formed with mafia money, the theft of public funding, and the money coming from the sale of stocks and from pension funds. This lumpen-bourgeoisie no longer respected any principle of legality, nor did it possess the strategic qualities of the protestant capitalism of the past. It was a baroque and cynical class, ready to use any means to seize power. In Russia, the Communist ruling class swiftly turned capitalist, while continuing its aggressive and authoritarian style of governing and exploiting social labor. In Italy, the new governing class emerged out of mafia money, the illegal seizure of an unbounded power over social communication, and the corruption of judges.

In the United States, for the first time in two hundred years, in the year 2000, we witnessed a phenomenon that was comparable to a *coup d'état*. After taking power, the new American president, George Bush, put forward an aggressively hegemonic policy. The first action of his presidency was to rip up the Kyoto agreements whereby industrialized countries had established a progressive reduction of toxic emissions in order to limit pollution and the effects of environmental devastation. The new president represented the interests of the great oil and weapons producers, who had economically sustained his electoral campaign. He also represented the interests of the ruling group of companies, like Enron, which have since fallen, after robbing the pension funds in which masses of employees had invested. The whole group sustaining Bush was implicated in the failure of American capitalism. Bush's power was founded on an alliance between old oil and the weapons economy, a failing and thieving lumpen-bourgeois class, and the private monopolies of information and communication, like Microsoft and Murdoch media.

As soon as the economic breakdown began, as if by miracle, three planes flew through the skies of Washington and New York. After the events of September 11, 2001 (S11), magically, the capitalism on the verge of bankruptcy could invest the energies of the whole society (which was displaying signs of exhaustion) in the direction of war. The general mobilization of these energies began with a call to a Holy War of the West against the evils of the world. Here begins the great Manichean campaign of Good versus Evil. The Good is represented by a group of oil magnates who have notoriously robbed public funds that led to the collapse of giant companies. Since the war on the Afghan population failed to produce any of the promised results, i.e. the arrest of the heads of the al-Qaeda organization accused of being responsible for the S11 attacks, the war must be relaunched. A new target is chosen: the former ally and accomplice Saddam Hussein is the target.

The motivations for a war on Iraq were ridiculous. "Saddam is an enemy of humanity." Of course, he already was one when he acted on behalf of the American administration and occupied Iran, just as many American allies have been, such as Sharon and the Saudi dynasty. "He used illegal weapons." As he did in 1988 with the financial and political support of the US. "He can make nuclear weapons." Which was improbable. Anyway, the violators of the nonproliferation treaty are multiple, starting with Israel. "We need to bring democracy to the Middle East." Nothing could have been more hypocritical. Democracy in the Middle East would require the departure of Israeli forces from the occupied territories and the recognition of the political rights of the Kurdish people. It would also mean reducing the role of the large oil corporations that, for fifty years, have been robbing the resources of those countries, while influencing their political life in a direct and authoritarian manner—starting with the CIA-sponsored military coup against Premier Mohammed Mossadeq in 1953, after he tried to nationalize the Iranian oil industry.

The ideology of security is the product of a paranoia fuelled by the media and geared to create an economic system of global security that can always feed on new paranoia. "We need to protect our quality of life." This was the only sentence that corresponded to truth in all the war propaganda: 20 percent of humanity did not wish to give up the consumption of 80 percent of the world's resources.

What were the possible scenarios of war in Iraq at the time? One was a rapid victory for the aggressors, the capture and trial of Baghdad's criminal, the imposition of a relatively peaceful protectorate, the American democratization of the Middle East, the progressive clearance of conflict zones, the imposition of a planetary military dictatorship for good purposes. But did anyone believe this to be possible? The more realistic scenario entailed the possibility of a fall of the Pakistani regime with Islamic fundamentalists getting ahold of two hundred nuclear warheads. The most probable consequence of aggression against Iraq was the explosion of Empire, the inauguration of the Empire of Chaos.

Meanwhile, something came to change the whole scenario: in the framework of a paranoid clash between fundamentalist and nationalist fanaticism and nazi-capitalist fanaticism, a *third actor* finally emerged, which we had been waiting for since S11 and which had been built with the stubborn labor of the global movement against corporations. The third actor came into being on February 15, 2003, as millions upon millions marched in cities around the globe to protest the war in Iraq. It was the movement of global everyday life rebelling against war-mongering dementia. What we saw on F15 was a movement destined to expand and radicalize. But when it does, it will be a matter of linking the process of exiting the war to the dissolution of the neoliberal domination of global capitalism, reposing the dynamic of anticapitalist conflict in society. Capitalism brings war as clouds bring storms, but in the course of war, the conditions for a redislocation of capitalism are created. The question of subverting the forces that produced the war is then posed. At that point, it won't be sufficient to eliminate the criminal class that produced the war. We'll need to clarify that war is only the continuation of neoliberal devastation by other means. Hence, it will be necessary to cut the roots of the process that leads to catastrophe.

AFTER THE DOTCOM CRASH

In the last decade of the century, the Web emerged as the essential support of the long expansive phase of digital capitalism. Millions of Americans and Europeans started to invest their money, buying and selling stocks from their own homes. The whole financial system became tightly interconnected. Nevertheless, the Web, this fantastic multiplier of popular participation in the market, risks intensifying its crises, and becoming the flight path from the media-financial system of control.

Another side of the process needs to be emphasized. Due to mass participation in the cycle of financial investment in the 1990s, a vast process of self-organization of cognitive producers got underway. Cognitive workers invested their expertise, their knowledge, and their creativity, and found in the stock market the means to create their own enterprises. For several years, the dotcom entrepreneurial form was the point where financial capital and highly productive cognitive labor met.

The libertarian and liberal ideology that dominated (American) cyberculture of the 1990s idealized the market by presenting it as a pure, almost mathematical environment. In this environment, as natural as the struggle for the survival of the fittest that makes evolution possible, labor would find the necessary means to valorize itself and become entrepreneurial. Once left to its own dynamic, the reticular economic system was destined to optimize economic gains for everyone, owners and workers alike—in part because the distinction between owners and workers would become increasingly imperceptible in the virtual productive circuit.

This model—imagined by authors such as Kevin Kelly and transformed by *Wired* magazine into a sort of digital-liberal, scornful, and emphatic *Weltanschauung*—went bankrupt in the first couple of years of the new millennium, along with the new economy and a large part of the army of self-employed cognitive entrepreneurs who had inhabited the dotcom world.

It went bankrupt because the model of a perfectly free market is a practical and theoretical lie. What neoliberalism supported in the long run was not the free market, but monopoly. While the market was idealized as a free space where knowledge, expertise, and creativity meet, reality showed that the large command centers operate in a way that far from being libertarian, introduce technological automatisms, impose themselves with the power of the media or money, and finally shamelessly rob the mass of shareholders and cognitive laborers.

The free market lie was exposed by the Bush administration. Its policy was one of explicit favoritism for monopolies (starting with the scandalous absolution of Bill Gates). It was a protectionist policy imposing open markets on weak states, while allowing the United States to impose 40 percent import taxes on steel.

Geert Lovink's 2002 book, *Dark Fiber*, contains a critique of this mixture of neoliberalism and protectionism from the point of view of net culture. This book is the first investigation of global net culture, an analysis of the evolution and involution of the Web during the first decade of its mass expansion. Lovink goes beyond a sociological, economic, and anthropological survey. Many of the essays in the book outline the theoretical positions of various agents in the cybercultural scene: *Wired*'s libertarian ideology, its economistic and neoliberal involution, and the radical pessimism of European philosophers. Lovink does not dwell on American neoliberal ideology, the defeated enemy. Instead, he invites us to understand what happened at the level of production in the years of dotcom mania.

We have no reason to cheer over the dotcom crash, he says. The ideology that characterized dotcom mania was a fanatical representation of obligatory optimism and economistic fideism. But the real process that developed in these years contained elements of social as well as technological innovation: elements that we should recuperate and re-actualize. In the second half of the 1990s, a real class struggle occurred within the productive circuit of high technologies. The becoming of the Web is still characterized by this struggle—and its outcome, at present, is unclear. Surely, the ideology of a free and natural market turned out to be a blunder. The idea that the market functions as a pure environment of equal confrontation among ideas, projects, and the productive quality and utility of services has been wiped out by the sour truth of monopolies waging war against the multitude of self-employed cognitive workers and the slightly pathetic mass of microtraders.

The struggle for survival was not won by the best and most successful; rather, it was won by the first to draw their gun—the gun of violence, robbery, systematic theft, and the violation of any legal or ethical norm. The Bush-Gates alliance sanctioned the liquidation of the market, and at that point the internal struggle of the virtual class ended. One part of the virtual class entered the technomilitary complex; another part (the large majority) was expelled from the industry and pushed to the margins of explicit proletarianization. On the cultural plane, the conditions for the formation of a social consciousness among the cognitariat are emerging, and this could be the most important phenomenon of the coming years, the solution to the disaster. Rather than a virtual class, I prefer to speak about a cognitive proletariat ("cognitariat") in order to emphasize the material (I mean physical, psychological, neurological) disease of the workers involved in the net economy.

Dotcoms have been the training laboratory for a productive model and a market. In the end, the market was conquered and suffocated by monopolies, and the army of self-employed entrepreneurs and venture microcapitalists was robbed and dissolved. A new phase began: the groups that became predominant in the cycle of the net economy forged an alliance with the dominant group of the old economy (the Bush clan, representative of the oil and military industry), which blocked the project of globalization. Neoliberalism produced its own negation, and those who were its most enthusiastic supporters became its victims.

Because of the dotcom crash of the year 2000, cognitive labor separated itself from capital. The alliance was broken. Digital artisans, who during the 1990s felt like entrepreneurs of their own labor, slowly realized that they had been deceived, expropriated, and this created the conditions for a new consciousness among cognitive workers.

Starting from these experiences, we need to rethink the old question of the intellectual that played such a crucial role in the nineteenth century. In the Leninist vision, the intellectual was considered a preindustrial actor, whose function was determined on the basis of a choice of organic affiliation with a social class. The Leninist party is the professional formation of intellectuals who choose to serve the proletarian cause. Antonio Gramsci introduced the notion of cultural hegemony—the specific work of ideology necessary to the process of seizing political power. But Gramsci remained fundamentally attached to an idea of the intellectual as an unproductive figure, an idea of culture as pure consensus with ideological values. The industrialization of culture that developed during the 1900s modified these figures, and critical theory realized this when it migrated from Frankfurt to Hollywood.

Benjamin and Marcuse, Adorno and Horkheimer, Brecht and Kracauer registered this passage. But it isn't until the digital Web redefined the whole process of production that intellectual labor assumed the configuration that Marx (1973, 706) had, in the *Grundrisse*, defined as "general intellect."

Pierre Lévy calls it collective intelligence; Derrick De Kerkhove points out that it actually is a connective intelligence. The infinitely fragmented mosaic of cognitive labor becomes a fluid process within a universal telematic network, and thus the shape of labor and capital are redefined. Capital becomes the generalized semiotic flux that runs through the veins of the global economy, while labor becomes the constant activation of the intelligence of countless semiotic agents linked to one another. Retrieving the concept of "general intellect" in the 1990s, Italian postworkerist or compositionist thought (Paolo Virno, Christian Marazzi, Maurizio Lazzarato, Carlo Formenti) introduced the concept of mass intellectuality, and emphasized the interaction between labor and language.

We had to go through the dotcom purgatory, through the illusion of a fusion between labor and capitalist enterprise, and then through the effects of the dotcom crash, in order to see the problem of labor emerge in new terms as immaterial and cognitive.

THE FUZZY ECONOMY OF COGNITIVE LABOR

Is it still possible to speak of Economics as a science when the production process is becoming immaterial, unstable, and unpredictable, and seems to elude the rules of computation that are at the core of the economic conceptual system? Peter Drucker writes:

Keynes, the post-Keynesians, and the neoclassicists alike cast the economy in a model in which a few constants drive the entire machinery. The model we now need would have to see the economy as "ecology," "environment," "configuration," and as composed of several integrative spheres: a "micro economy" of individuals and firms, especially transnational ones; a "macro economy" of national governments; and a world economy. Every earlier economic theory postulated that one such economy totally controls; all others are dependent and "functions." But economic reality now is one of three such economies. None of them totally controls the other two; none is totally controlled by the others. Yet none is fully independent from the others, either. Such complexity can barely be described. It cannot be analyzed since it allows of no prediction. To give us a functioning economic theory, we thus need a new synthesis that simplifies—but so far there is no sign of it. And if no such synthesis emerges, we might be at the end of economic theory. (Drucker 1989, 156–7).

Economics became a science when, with the expansion of capitalism, rules were established as general principles for productive activity and exchange. But if we want these rules to function we must be able to quantify the basic productive act. The time-atom described by Marx is the keystone of modern economics. Calculating the time necessary for the production of a commodity makes possible the regulation of the entire set of economic relations. But when the main element in the global productive cycle is the unforeseeable work of the mind, the unforeseeable work of language, when self-reproducing information becomes the universal commodity, it's no longer possible to reduce the totality of exchanges and relations to an economic rule.

Drucker continues:

In any system as complex as the economy of a developed country, the statistically insignificant events, the events at the margin, are likely to be the decisive events, short range at least. By definition they can neither be anticipated nor prevented. Indeed, they cannot always be identified even after they have had their impact. (Drucker 1989, 166).

Economic science is founded on a quantitative and mechanistic paradigm that can comprehend and regulate industrial production, the physical manipulation of mechanical matter. But it is unable to explain and regulate the process of immaterial production based on activities that can't easily be reduced to quantitative measurements and the repetition of constants: mental activity.

Due to the new technologies, Jacques Robin (1989, 39) explains, even the concept of productivity fails to resist the challenge raised by new realities like economic growth without job creation. With the new technologies, most production costs are determined by research and equipment expenses that actually precede the productive process. Little by little, in digitalized and automated enterprises, production is no longer subject to variations in the *quantity* of operational factors. Marginal cost, marginal profits: these bases of neoclassical economic calculations have lost a good part of their meaning. The traditional elements of wage and price calculation are crumbling.

Mental work is not computable in precise and predictable terms like the work performed by an industrial worker. Therefore, the determination of value—the keystone of classical economy both as a science and as daily economic practice—becomes aleatory and indefinable. "Realist" economies (economies based on a computable amount of labor time) were governed by their goals: the naïve goal of producing use value for the satisfaction of specific needs, or the subtler goal of valorization as the increase of invested capital. Now, instead, it's impossible to explain our economies on the basis of their goals, whether we identify them with the intentions of certain individuals or groups, or with the goals of an entire society. The economy is governed by a code, not by its goals:

> Finality is there in advance, inscribed in the code. The order of goals has simply ceded its place to a molecular play, as the order of signifieds has yielded to the play of infinitesimal signifiers, reduced to their aleatory commutation. (Baudrillard 1993a: 59).

In Baudrillard's vision, the economy therefore appears as a hyperreality, a simulated, double, an artificial world that cannot be translated in terms of real production. Consequently, economic science can no longer explain the fundamental dynamics governing humanity's productive activities; nor can it explain their crisis. Economics has to be replaced by a global science whose characteristics and field of inquiry are still unknown: a science that would be able to study the processes that form cyberspace, the global network of signs-commodities.

In an interview published in 1993 by *Wired*, Peter Drucker expands on the theme of the inadequacy of economic categories associated with the digitalization of production:

> International economic theory is obsolete. The traditional factors of production—land, labor, and capital—are becoming restraints rather than driving forces. Knowledge is becoming the one critical factor of production. It has two incarnations: knowledge applied to existing processes, services, and products is productivity; knowledge applied to the new is innovation. [...] Knowledge has become the central, key resource that knows no geography. It underlies the most significant and unprecedented social phenomenon of this century. No class in history has ever risen as fast as the blue-collar worker and no class has fallen as fast. All within less than a century. (Drucker, in Schwartz 1992, n.p.).

Furthermore, Drucker remarks that the concept of intellectual property, which is a juridical concept at the root of classical economics and the capitalist system, no longer has any meaning in an age when the circulating commodity is information and the market is the infosphere:

> We have to rethink the whole concept of intellectual property, which was focused on the printed word. Perhaps within a few decades, the distinction between electronic transmissions and the printed word will have disappeared. The only solution may be a universal licensing system. Where you basically become a subscriber, and where it's taken for granted that everything that is published is reproduced. In other words, if you don't want everybody to know, don't talk about it. (*Ibid*).

As a conclusion to these observations on the obsolescence of economics as a generalized interpretive code, I would like to quote André Gorz, who writes in his *Metamorphoses du travail*:

Discipline by means of money is a hetero-regulation that interrupts the communicational infrastructure ensuring the symbolic reproduction of the experiential world. This means that all the activities that transmit or reproduce cultural acquisitions, knowledge, taste, manners, language, mores [...], and that allow us to find our bearings in the world as givens, certitudes, values, and self-explanatory norms; all these activities cannot be regulated by money or by the state without causing serious pathologies in our world of experience. (Gorz 1988, 132).

Money (i.e. economics) and the State (i.e. politics) are no longer able to govern or discipline the world of production, now that its center is not a de-brained force, a uniform and quantifiable time of manual work. That center is now occupied by mind flows, by the ethereal substance of intelligence, which eludes every measurement and cannot be subjected to any rule without inducing enormous pathologies and causing a truly maddening paralysis of cognition and affectivity.

INFOLABOR AND PRECARIZATION

We have no future because our present is too volatile. The only possibility that remains is the management of risk. The spinning top of the scenarios of the present moment.
—William Gibson, *Pattern Recognition*

In February 2003, the American journalist Bob Herbert published in the *New York Times* the results of a cognitive survey of hundreds of unemployed youths in Chicago: none of the interviewees expected to find work in the next few years; none expected to be able to rebel, or set off large-scale collective change. The general sense of the interviews was a sentiment of profound impotence. The perception of decline did not seem focused on politics, but on a deeper cause, a scenario of social and psychic involution that seemed to cancel every possibility of building alternatives. During the zero zero decade, precariousness has spread throughout the organization of labor, becoming the prevailing feeling of the new generation.

The fragmentation of the present is reversed in the implosion of the future.

In *The Corrosion of Character: The Transformation of Work in Modern Capitalism*, Richard Sennett reacts to this existential condition of precariousness and fragmentation with nostalgia for a past epoch in which life was structured in relatively stable social roles, and time had enough linear consistency to construe paths of identity: "Time's arrow is broken; it has no trajectory in a continually re-engineered, routine-hating, short-term political economy. People feel the lack of sustained human relations and durable purposes" (Sennett 1998, 98).

But this nostalgia has no hold on present reality, and attempts to reactivate the community remain artificial and sterile.

Precariousness is itself a precarious notion, because it defines its object in an approximate manner, but also because from this notion derive paradoxical, self-contradictory, in other words precarious strategies. If we concentrate our critical attention on the precarious character of job performance, what kind of program can we propose, to what target can we aspire? That of a stable job guaranteed for life? This would be (and actually is) a cultural regression, the definite subordination of labor to the rule of exploitation. Notwithstanding the idea of "flexicurity," we are still far from any strategy of social recomposition of the labor movement that might extricate us from unlimited exploitation. We need to pick up again the thread of analysis of social composition and decompositon if we want to discern possible outlines of any recomposition to come.

In the 1970s, the energy crisis, the consequent economic recession, and finally the replacement of workers with numerical machines resulted in a large number of people with no guarantees. The question of precariousness soon became central to social analysis, but also to the ambitions of the movement. We began by proposing to struggle for forms of guaranteed income, not linked to work, in order to face the fact that a large part of the young population had no prospect of guaranteed employment. The situation has changed since then, because what seemed a marginal and temporary condition has now become the prevalent form of labor relations. Precariousness is no longer a marginal and provisional characteristic, but it is the general form of the labor relation in a productive, digitalized sphere, reticular and recombinant.

The word "precariat" generally stands for work that no longer has fixed rules about labor relations, salary, or the length of the work day. However, if we analyze the past, we see that these rules functioned only for a limited period in the history of relations between labor and capital. Only for a short period at the heart of the twentieth century, under the political pressures of unions and workers, in conditions of (almost) full employment, and thanks to a generally strong regulatory role played by the state in the economy, some limits to the natural violence of capitalist dynamics could be legally established. The legal obligations that in certain periods have protected society from the violence of capital were always founded on political and material relations of force (workers' violence against the violence of capital). Thanks to political force, it became possible to affirm rights, establish laws, and protect them as personal rights. With the decline in the political force of the workers' movement, the natural precariousness and brutality of labor relations in capitalism have re-emerged.

The new phenomenon is not the precarious character of the job market, but the technical and cultural conditions in which infolabor is made precarious. The technical conditions are based on digital recombination of infolabor in networks. The cultural conditions include the education of the masses and the expectations of consumption inherited from late twentieth century society, which are continuously fed by the entire apparatus of marketing and media communication.

If we analyze the first aspect, the technical transformations introduced by the digitalization of the productive cycle, we see that the essential point is not that the labor relation has become precarious (which, after all, it has always been), but the dissolution of the person as active productive agent, as labor power. The cyberspace of global production can be described as an immense expanse of depersonalized human time.

Infolabor, the provision of time for the elaboration and recombination of segments of infocommodities, takes to the extreme the tendency, which Marx analyzed, for labor to become abstracted from concrete activity.

This process of abstraction has progressively stripped labor time of every concrete and individual particularity. The atom of time of which Marx wrote is the minimal unit of productive labor. But in industrial production, abstract labor time was impersonated by a physical and juridical bearer, embodied in a worker in flesh and bone, with a certified and political identity. Naturally, capital did not purchase a personal disposition, but the time for which the workers were its bearers. But if capital wanted to dispose of the necessary time for its valorization, it was obliged to hire a human being, to buy all of its time, and therefore it had to face up to the material needs and the social and political demands of which the human was a bearer. When we move onto the sphere of infolabor, there is no longer a need to buy a person for eight hours a day indefinitely. Capital no longer recruits people, but buys packets of time, separated from their interchangeable and occasional bearers.

Depersonalized time has become the real agent of valorization, and depersonalized time has neither any right, nor any demand. It can only be either available or unavailable, but this is purely theoretical because the physical body, despite not being a legally recognized person, still has to buy food and pay rent.

The informatic procedures of the recombination of semiotic material have the effect of liquefying the "objective" time necessary to produce the infocommodity. In all of the time of life, the human machine is there, pulsating and available, like a brain-sprawl in waiting. The extension of time is meticulously cellularized: cells of productive time can be mobilized in punctual, casual, and fragmentary forms. The recombination of these fragments is automatically realized in the network. The mobile phone is the tool that makes possible the connection between the needs of semiocapital and the mobilization of the living labor of cyberspace. The ringtone of the mobile phone calls the workers to reconnect their abstract time to the reticular flux.

It's a strange word—"liberalism"—with which we identify the ideology prevalent in the posthuman transition to digital slavery. Liberty is its foundational myth, but the liberty of whom? The liberty of capital, certainly. Capital must be absolutely free to expand in every corner of the world to find the fragment of human time available to be exploited for the most miserable wage. But liberalism also predicates the liberty of the person. In neoliberal rhetoric, the juridical person is free to express itself, to choose representatives, and be entrepreneurial at the level of politics and the economy. All this is very interesting, except that the person has disappeared; what is left is like an inert object, irrelevant and useless. The person is free, sure. But his time is enslaved.

His liberty is a juridical fiction to which nothing in concrete daily life corresponds. If we consider the conditions in which the work of the majority of humanity, proletariat and cognitariat, is actually carried out in our time, if we examine the conditions of the average wage globally, if we consider the current cancellation of previous labor rights, we can say with no rhetorical exaggeration that we live in a regime of slavery. Globally, the average wage is hardly sufficient to buy the mere survival of a person whose time is at the service of capital. And people have no right over the time of which they are formally the proprietors, but from which they are effectively expropriated. That time does not really belong to them, because it is separated from the social existence of the people who make it available to the recombinant cyberproductive circuit. The time of work is fractalized, that is, reduced to minimal fragments for reassembly, and the fractalization makes it possible for capital to constantly find the conditions for the minimum wage.

Precariousness is the black heart of the capitalist production process in the global network, where a continuous flow of fragmented and recomposable infowork circulates. Precariousness is the transformative element of the whole cycle of production. Nobody is outside its reach. At unspecified times, workers' wages are reduced or cut, and the life of all is threatened. Digital infolabor can be fragmented in order to be recomposed someplace other than where that work is done.

From the point of view of the valorization of capital, flow is continuous, but from the point of view of the existence and time of cognitive workers, productive activity has the character of recombinant fragmentation in cellular form. Pulsating cells of work are lit and extinguished in the large control room of global production. Infolabor is innately precarious, not because of the contingent viciousness of employers but for the simple reason that the allocation of work time can be disconnected from the individual and legal person of the worker, an ocean of valorizing cells convened in a cellular way and recombined by the subjectivity of capital.

It is appropriate to reconceptualize the relationship between recombinant capital and immaterial labor, and it is advisable to obtain a new framework of reference. Given the impossibility, from now on, of reaching a contractual elaboration of the cost of work by basing it on the legal person—because productive abstract labor is disconnected from the individual person of the worker—the traditional form of the wage is no longer operative, since it can't guarantee anything anymore. Therefore, the recombinant character of cognitive labor seems incompatible with any possibility of social recomposition or subjectivation. The rules of negotiation, collaboration, and conflict have changed, not because of a political decision, but because of a technical and cultural change in the labor relationship. The rules are not immutable, and there is no rule which forces us to comply with the rules. The legalist Left has never understood this. Fixed on the idea that it is necessary to comply with the rules, it has never known how to carry out confrontation on the new ground inaugurated by digital technologies and the globalized cycle of infolabor. The neoliberals have understood this very well and they have subverted the rules that were laid down in a century of trade union history.

In the classical mode of industrial production, the rule was based on a rigid relationship between labor and capital, and on the possibility of determining the value of goods on the basis of socially necessary working time. But in the recombining stage of capital based on exploitation of fluid infowork, there is no longer any deterministic relation between labor and value.

We should not aim to restore the rules that neoliberal power has violated; we should invent new rules adequate to the fluid form of the labor-capital relation, where there is no longer any quantitative time-value determinism and, thus, where there is no longer any necessary constant in economic relations.

How can we oppose the systemic depersonalization of the working class and the slavery that is affirmed in the command of precarious and depersonalized work? This is the question that is posed with insistence by whomever still has a sense of human dignity. Nevertheless, no answer comes, because the forms of resistance and struggle that were efficacious in the twentieth century appear to no longer have the capacity to spread and consolidate, nor, consequently, can they stop the absolutism of capital.

We have learned from the experience of workers' struggle in recent years that the struggle of precarious workers does not become a cycle, does not leave a social sediment of consciousness, organization, and solidarity. Fractalized work can also intermittently rebel, but this does not set any wave of struggle in motion. The reason is easy to understand. In order for struggles to form a cycle there must be a spatial proximity of laboring bodies and an existential temporal continuity. Without this proximity and this continuity, we lack the conditions for cellularized bodies to become a community.

CITY OF PANIC

The urban territory is increasingly traversed by streams of diasporic, heterogeneous, and deterritorialized imaginaries. Panic tends to become the urban psychic dimension. It is the reaction of a sensitive organism subjected to stimulation that is too strong and too rapid. The reaction of an organism urged on by impulses too frequent and intense to be emotively and conversationally elaborated.

What is panic? We are told that psychiatrists recently discovered and named a new kind of disorder—they call it "Panic Disorder." It seems that it's something quite recent in the psychological self-perception of human beings. But what does panic mean? "Panic" used to be a nice word, and this is the sense in which the Swiss-American psychoanalyst James Hillman remembers it in his book on Pan. Pan was the god of nature and totality. In Greek mythology, Pan was the symbol of the relationship between man and nature. Nature is the overwhelming flow of reality, things, and information that surrounds us. Modern culture is based on the idea of human domination, which is the domestication of nature. So the original panic feeling (which was something positive to the ancient world) is becoming increasingly terrifying and destructive. Today, panic has become a form of psychopathology: we can speak of panic when we see a conscious organism (individual or social) overwhelmed by the speed of processes in which it is involved, and where it has insufficient time to handle the information generated by those processes.

Technological transformations have displaced the economic process from the sphere of the production of material goods toward the sphere of semiotic goods. With this, semiocapital becomes the dominant form of the economy. The accelerated creation of surplus value depends on the acceleration of the infosphere. The digitalization of the infosphere opens the way for this kind of acceleration. Signs are produced and circulated at a growing speed, but the human terminal of the system (the embodied mind) is put under growing pressure and finally cracks. I think that the current economic crisis has something to do with this imbalance between the fields of semioproduction and semiodemand. This imbalance between the supply of semiotic goods and the socially available time of attention is the core of the economic crisis as well as the core of the intellectual and the political crises we are living through now.

Semiocapital is in a crisis of overproduction, but the form of this crisis is not only economic, but also psychopathic. Semiocapital, in fact, is not about the production of material goods, but about the production of psychic stimulation. The mental environment is saturated by signs that create a sort of continuous excitation, a permanent electrocution, which leads the individual, as well as the collective mind, to a state of collapse.

The problem of panic is generally associated with the management of time. But we can also see a spatial side to panic. During past centuries, the building of the modern urban environment used to be dependent on the rationalist plan of the political city. The economic dictatorship of the last few decades has accelerated urban expansion. The interaction between cyberspatial sprawl and the urban physical environment has destroyed the rational organization of city space.

At the intersection of information and urban space, we see the proliferation of a chaotic sprawl following no rule, no plan, dictated solely by the logic of economic interest. Urban panic is caused by the perception of this sprawl and this proliferation of metropolitan experience. Proliferation of spatial lines of flight. The metropolis is a surface of complexity in the territorial domain. The social organism is unable to process the overwhelmingly complex experience of metropolitan chaos. The proliferation of lines of communication has created a new kind of chaotic perception.

In the summer of 2001, *Fury*, a novel by Salman Rushdie, was published. On the cover, the Empire State building is hit by a bolt of lightning. Not long after its release, that cover looked like a frightening premonition. But this premonition was not just on the cover, for the novel describes (or rather evokes) the psychic collapse of the western metropolis. Rushdie depicts the virtual class nervous system, a social class of producers of signs as well as a class of people living a common condition of evanescence and existential fragility: cellularized splinters, fragments in a perpetual abstract recombination of connected terminals. You feel the psychopathic vibration that is building, after the decade of permanent electrocution, the decade of frenzied economic investment. You feel anxiety growing, and the urban libidinal economy going insane.

Millions of mobile phones are calling each other, mobilizing libidinal energy, postponing contact, the pleasure of orgasm, from one side of the city to the other, from one moment of compressed urban time to another.

The action of Rushdie's novel develops mainly on the roofs of Manhattan skyscrapers. Scary black birds wondering about the fates of buildings announce the next collapse.

Some time ago, Mike Davis investigated the urban territorial perception of Los Angeles, in *City of Quartz* (1990), and New York City, in *Dead Cities* (2003). He mapped the construction of the mythologies of fear, security, and privatization policies that have a devastating effect on social space. For Davis: "The neomilitary syntax of contemporary architecture insinuates violence and averts imaginary threats. The pseudopublic spaces of today, the big malls and the executive centers, the cultural acropolis and so on are full of invisible signs to keep the underclass far away" (Davis 1990, 226).

After S11, the securitization paranoia became the main tendency in the imaginary, in the production of high technology goods, and in urban design. Again, Davis writes:

> The fear economy grows in the middle of an overall famine.... The low paid security guard army will grow by 50% during the decade, while video-surveillance fed by facial recognition software will snatch what is left of privacy from the daily routine. The airports' departure security regime will provide a model for the regulation of the urban masses, in the shopping centers, in the sporting events and elsewhere.... Security, in other words, will become an urban service completely developed like water, electricity and telecommunications. (Davis 2003, 12–13).

In the city of panic, there is no longer time to get close to each other; there is no more time for caresses, for the pleasure and slowness of whispered words. Advertising exalts and stimulates the libidinous attention, person-to-person communication multiplies the promises of encounters, but these promises never get fulfilled. Desire turns into anxiety, and time contracts.

chapter three

BAROQUE

AND

SEMIOCAPITAL

SINCETHEDAWN

of the modern age in the sixteenth and seventeenth centuries, says Bolivar Echeverria in *Vuelta de siglo* [*Turn of the Century*] (2006), there have been two modernities, conflicting and interweaving.

The first is the prevailing bourgeois vision of modernity based on the Protestant ethic and a strong belief that what counts in life is the product of material labor. The other vision of modernity was nurtured in the Catholic Counter-Reformation, and in the sensibility of the Baroque. This second modernity was denied and marginalized when the industrialization of the human environment reduced the social field to a process of mechanization.

The life of the industrial bourgeoisie was based on strict dedication to tireless labor, and on proprietary affection toward its products. The bourgeoisie is strongly territorialized because the accumulation of value cannot be dissociated from the expansion of physical things produced by the conflictive cooperation of workers' manual skills and capitalists' financial skills.

Echeverria remarks that, since the sixteenth century, the Catholic Church has created a different stream of modernity, based on the immaterial skills of imagination and on the potencies of deterritorialization. The spiritual power of Rome has always been based on the control of minds: this is its capital, although this was harshly opposed by the pragmatic ethics of industrial culture.

Catholic Spain in the sixteenth and seventeenth centuries was the harbinger of a nonindustrial brand of accumulation, based on massive robbery of the new territories discovered and conquered across the Atlantic Ocean. This cultural stream of modernity was marginalized after the military defeat of the "Invincible Armada" in the naval war with the British Empire and the subsequent economic decline of Spain. The triumph of Northern European capitalism opens the way to the Industrial Revolution and the creation of the material sphere of Indust-Reality. But the Baroque cultural stream of modernity was not erased, it never stopped working underground in the modern imaginary, and it resurfaces at last, when the capitalist system changes its social nature and its imagination at the end of the twentieth century. Postmodern imagination can be considered a resurgence of the Baroque spirit, and the centrality of semiotic production in the sphere of the economy is the main mark of postmodern society.

In his beautiful book *Images at War*, whose telling subtitle is *From Columbus to Blade Runner*, Serge Gruzinski recapitulates the history of the hybrid-mestizo Baroque imagination from the times of the Spanish conquest of the Mexican lands to the Hollywood age. "The mannerist and then baroque image played with decorative loading, allegorical flowering, the pursuit of wisdom, sophistication, and a multiplicity of meaning" (Gruzinski 2001, 114).

This sensibility permeated the surrealist and psychedelic imagination, and deeply penetrated Californian late-modern culture, helping create the hypervisual infosphere that prevailed in the age of movies and TV. In the video-electronic sphere, images are no longer a pure representation of reality, they become simulation and psychophysical stimulation of the social brain, taking central place in the world of the commodity. Signs are not only goods that can be produced and exchanged with money. They become the universal merchandise, the general equivalent in economic perception. In a vertiginous turn, immaterial signs take the place of physicals things, as the main object of capitalist valorization. And so, if the territorialized bourgeois economy was based on the iconoclastic severity of iron and steel, postmodern deterritorialization is based instead on the kaleidoscopic machine of semiotic production. This is why we can speak of semiocapitalism: because the goods that are circulating in the economic world—informational, financal, imaginary—are signs, figures, images, projections, expectations.

Language is no longer a tool for representing the economic process. It becomes the main source of accumulation, constantly deterritorializing the field of exchange. Speculation and spectacle intermingle, because of the intrinsic inflationary (metaphoric) nature of language. The linguistic web of semioproduction is a game of mirrors that inevitably leads to crises of overproduction, bubbles and bursts.

We need to see the social implications of the two different streams of modernity: the relationship between the industrial bourgeoisie and the working class has been based on conflict, but also on alliance and mutual cooperation. The dynamics of progress and growth, stemming from the territorial physical space of the factory, forced an agreement between the two fundamental classes of industrial times, industrial workers and industrial bourgeoisie. This agreement was based on collective negotiation and the creation of the Welfare State. The bourgeoisie and working class could not dissociate their destinies, despite the radical conflict opposing wages and profit, living time and time of valorization.

The ideology of dialectics, especially in the totalitarian vision of Leninist Communism, broke this alliance between bourgeoisie and worker, and turned the social history of the century into a radical split between capitalist temporality and Soviet Communist temporality.

This dialectical polarization and stiffening of social conflict into a form of identitarian, institutional, and military antagonism provoked a catastrophic turn in the history of social emancipation and the prospects for social autonomy. The dialectical ideology did not interpret workers' interests, did not understand the complexity of the relationship between social struggle and technological progress. This forced social struggle into a conceptual trap, which wasn't broken until 1989, when the potency of social autonomy all over the world was already exhausted and dissolving under the effects of technological restructuring.

Since the 1970s, the relation between capital and labor has been reframed, thanks to the new digital technology and to the deregulation of the labor market. The result was a massive deterritorialization, and the very foundation of the classical bourgeois worldview was swept away, along with the old workers' class consciousness. The financialization of the global economy has eroded the bourgeois identification of wealth with physical property and territorial labor. When labor loses its mechanical form and becomes immaterial, linguistic, and affective, the deterministic relation between time and value is broken. The generation of value enters a phase of indeterminacy and uncertainty. The way is cleared for the arrival of a neo-Baroque vision of the world, and the establishment of an aleatory logic in the heart of economy: Deregulation.

A new alliance between labor and capital became possible in the last decade of the twentieth century. The experience of dotcom enterprises was the expression of this alliance, which allowed the extraordinary technological progress of the digital sphere. But this alliance is broken when criminal behavior fills the vacuum of the aleatory. When language becomes the general field of production, when the mathematical relation of labor time and value is broken, when deregulation destroys all liabilities, a criminal class takes the lead. This is what has happened since neoliberal politics has occupied the world scene. The first principle of the neoliberal school, deregulation that destroys political and legal limits to capitalist expansion, cannot be understood as a purely political change. It has to be seen in the context of technological and cultural evolution, which have displaced the process of valorization from mechanical industry to semiotic production. The relation between labor time and valorization becomes uncertain, undeterminable. Cognitive labor is hardly reducible to the measure of time. It's impossible to determine how much social time is necessary for the production of an idea. When the relation between labor and value becomes indeterminable, the pure law of violence, of abuse, reigns in the global labor market. No more simple exploitation, but slavery, pure violence against the vulnerable lives of global workers.

Violence has become the prevailing economic force in the neoliberal age. Violence of the Italian, Mexican, Russian organizations that command the market of narcotics, weapons, prostitution, and that invest in the financial market. Call it mafia or whatever. In Mexico as in Italy as in Russia, financial markets, mediascapes, and political power are in the hands of people who gained power through lawlessness and violence.

And this is not to mention the role of corporations like Halliburton or Blackwater (now Xe) in the US: fuelling wars and destroying lives, jeopardizing countries because this is their business, a business that needs war.

The neo-Baroque theater of cruelty is the effect of semiodominance in the sphere of social production. The Italian experience during the last hundred years has been the main theater of this return of the Baroque spirit. Both Mussolini's and Berlusconi's performances are based on the theatrical exhibition of macho energy, but also on the ability to penetrate into the recesses of language, in the deep field of self-perception.

The feminine side of Italian self-perception is at stake in both cases. Mussolini and the young Futurists of 1909 wanted to despise, possess, and subordinate women's bodies. Berlusconi and the lumpen who surround him (pimps, media bootlickers, lawyers) want to soil women's bodies; they want to inject self-hatred into every cell of the social body.

LUMPEN ITALIAN

Looking at the Italian scene one might think that this country is a fanciful place where craziness reigns and corrupt behavior melds with irresponsibility, a place that doesn't have much to do with the general history of postmodern capitalist becoming. But the truth is quite different. While strange, the Italian scene has often been the laboratory of the new avatars of capitalist power. Think of Mussolini's dictatorship; although farcical, it was the beginning of a dramatic turning point in the history of power and social imagination. So, please don't laugh when you think about Berlusconi's comedy. It's not only the return of the *commedia dell'arte*; it could also prefigure a new wave in the power of management, the expression of the new class leading the economy everywhere, what I call the lumpen-bourgeoisie, after the description of Roberto Saviano's 2007 book *Gomorrah*.

The lumpen-bourgeoisie has lost the virtues of the old bourgeoisie: thrift, attachment to property, and attention to human industriousness. The *affectio societatis* of the old entrepreneur has disappeared. The new capitalist does not build his fortune on local enterprise, but on aleatory financial investment that has no relationship to territory or the living local community.

The concept of competition has replaced that of competence. Competence is the intellectual skill that enabled the bourgeoisie to carry out its planning, administrative, and organizational function, and justified its right to property. But in financial capitalism the competent bourgeoisie of the past has been replaced by a class that turned competition into the only rule. As property came to coincide with a dusty cloud of fragmentary investments rather than with any person, competition replaced competence. Many competences are still necessary to production, but they are now detached from the role of the enterprise. Any intellectual competence that is not related to speculation is made precarious, devalued, and low waged.

Only those who have become very skilled in managerial functions can become wealthy through their labor. What does a managerial function detached from the specificity of concrete intellectual competence consist of? Fabrication, trickery, lies and fraudulent accounting, tax evasion, and, if necessary, the physical removal of competitors, torture, and genocide. In this respect, Halliburton is more efficient and heinous than the Sicilian mafia and the Neapolitan camorra.

Ignorance rises to power and economic decisions are made purely on the basis of the maximum and most immediate profit. All that matters is the reduction of labor costs, because this is what competition is about—it has nothing to do with the production of quality. As a result, the last word on decisions about production does not come from chemists, urban planners, or doctors, but from people with managerial competence, that is, with the ability to reduce labor costs and accelerate the realization of profit. The dynamics of neoliberalism have destroyed the bourgeoisie and replaced it with two distinct and opposing classes: the cognitariat on the one hand, i.e., the precarious and cellularized labor of intelligence, and the managerial class on the other, whose only competence is in competitiveness. Taken to its extreme, as evident in increasingly larger regions of global capitalist production, competition becomes the armed removal of competitors, the armed imposition of one supplier, the systematic devastation of everything that does not submit to the profit of the strongest. Who competes better than those who eliminate their competitors? And what better techniques for this removal exist than burying people alive, slaughtering or dissolving them in muriatic acid? Gomorrah is inscribed in the genetic code of neoliberalism.

The neoliberal phase of capitalism appears to be an interminable and uninterrupted process of deregulation, but in fact it's the exact opposite. As all rules of coexistence are abolished, the rules of violence are imposed. As the regulations that limited the invasiveness of competitive principles are removed, hard and fast automatisms are introduced in material relations between people, who become more enslaved as the enterprise becomes freer. The process of deregulation unremittingly removes the rules that bridle the mobility of productivity and hinder the expansive power of capital. Forms of social civilization and human rights established throughout modernity are rules that deregulation wants to eliminate. One by one, the advance of capitalist deregulation eradicates the cultural and juridical conventions of modernity and bourgeois law. This is why capitalism has turned into a criminal system and keeps working toward the expansion of the realm of pure violence, where its advancement can proceed unhindered. *Slatterkapitalismus*: the end of bourgeois hegemony and of the enlightened universality of the law.

Crime is no longer a marginal function of the capitalist system, but the decisive winning factor for deregulated competition. Torture, homicide, child exploitation, the drive to prostitution, and production of instruments of mass destruction have become irreplaceable techniques of economic competition.

LANGUAGE AND POISON

"When *I* use a word ... it means just what I choose it to mean—neither more nor less... The question is ... which [meaning] is to be master—that's all," says Lewis Carroll's (1971, 56) Humpty Dumpty, recognizing straightaway, like a good master, that when you ask words to do overtime, you have to pay them more.

And Deleuze (1990, 18), who refers to Humpty Dumpty in the third series of *The Logic of Sense*, titled "Of the Proposition," comments: "the last recourse seems to be identifying sense with signification." Not sense, but the activity of producing meaning through the innumerable shifts and slides that this process involves. In order to speak of the Italian *dérive* of the last fifteen years we must begin from a semiotic of transgression and of sliding.

The word "*dérive*" scares those who believe politics must respect a set of rules and that law must be the center of social life, those who think that words have only one meaning, and that to understand one another in life it's necessary to use words according to their established meanings. This is all wrong. When we speak, we don't respect the meanings of words but invent them. Understanding is not the exchange of signs supplied with a univocal referent. To understand is to follow the slides in the relations between signs and referents, reinventing signs as functions of new referents and creating new referents by circulating new signs. Similarly politics does not have to respect any one law, because it invents the law when it creates new relations.

Following rules is a good thing, but politics cannot be reduced to this, because there is no rule that says that rules must be respected. Berlusconi understood this, and he won all that he could possibly win. The Left did not understand it and finally vanished, to leave space, let's hope, for a new social autonomy capable of inventing new words, new referents, and above all, new forms of relations.

One night in October 1977 while the fires of the student riots were dying out, Silvio Berlusconi met Mike Buongiorno, a man who had been featured on the screen since the beginning of Italian television. They dined together in a Milan restaurant and, out of their simple minds, an extraordinary linguistic machine was born, capable of a mutagenetic biopolitical penetration of the Italian brain. Since then, Berlusconi's capital has operated in a perfectly recombinatory manner:

having built its financial base on estates, it invested in advertising, insurance, football, and television. To put this enormous conglomerate into motion, Berlusconi, who was a member of the secret society P2 and friends with characters like Marcello Dell'Utri, who reeked of the mafia, violated many of the laws of the Italian Republic: cooking the books, corrupting judges, conflicts of interest. For twenty years he outmaneuvered magistrates, journalists, and institutions that accused him of breaking the law. But what is the law? A linguistic effect that dissolves as common sense changes. In three decades, common sense has changed because Berlusconi's media machine has inoculated linguistic substances in perfect doses to produce white noise.

Far from being a backward phenomena or a transitory anomaly, the Berlusconi phenomenon is a sign of things to come, well actually, a time that has already arrived. Over the last few decades, an infrastructure for the engineering of the psychosphere was constituted, one that could modulate public mood and produce opinion, but above all, that was capable of destroying psychic sensibility and the empathetic sociability of the new generations, who were induced to mistake the uninterrupted flow of television for "the world."

Contemporary capitalism can be defined as semiocapitalism because the general shape of commodities has a semiotic character and the process of production is increasingly the elaboration of sign-information. In the sphere of semiocapital, economic production is increasingly tightly interwoven with processes of linguistic exchange, as is explained clearly in the books of Christian Marazzi and those of Paulo Virno.

Thanks to language, we can create shared worlds, formulate ambiguous enunciations, elaborate metaphors, simulate events, or simply lie. Semio-economics is the creation of worlds, castles of metaphors, imagination, predictions, simulations, and fabrications. What better country than the one that gave us *commedia dell' arte* could insert itself in a productive system based on chatter, spectacle, and exhibition?

The Fordist industrial economy was founded on the production of objectively measurable value quantifiable by socially necessary labor time. The postindustrial economy is based on linguistic exchange, on the value of simulation. This simulation becomes the decisive element in the determination of value. And when simulation becomes central to the productive process, lies, deceit, and fraud enter to play a part in economic life, not as exceptional transgressions of the norm but as laws of production and exchange.

The laws of semiocapital don't resemble those of the glorious epoch of industry; its relations don't involve the productive discipline, work ethic, or enterprise that dominated the world of classical industrial capitalism, the Protestant capitalism that Michel Albert (1993) dubs "of the Rhine." A deep transformation has taken place in the last few decades, starting from the separation of the financial circuit from the real economy.

The founding act of this separation was Nixon's arbitrary decision to abandon the Bretton Woods system. In 1971, the American President decided to rescind the rules on the convertibility of the dollar into gold and to thus affirm the self-referentiality of the American standard. Despite the implications of Vietnam, at this time American power still had credibility and the strength to impose its decisions as if they were objective and incontrovertible. Today, that power and credibility have dissolved, the value of the dollar has fallen, and the economy of simulation has thus entered into a phase of instability.

From the moment Nixon told the world of the decision to unhook the dollar from every gauge of objectivity, money fully became what it already was in essence: a pure act of language. No longer a referential sign that relates to a mass of commodities, a quantity of gold, or to some other objective data, money now relates to a factor of simulation, an agent capable of putting into motion arbitrary processes independent of the real economy. Therefore, semiocapital is a system of complete indeterminacy: financialization and immaterialization have brought to the relations between social actors unpredictability and chance elements never seen before in the history of the industrial economy. In Fordist industrial production, the determination of the value of a commodity was founded on a specific factor: the socially necessary labor time to produce it. But in semiocapitalism this is no longer true. When the main feature of commodity production is cognitive labor, the labor of attention, memory, language, and imagination, the criteria of value are no longer objective and cannot be quantified on the basis of a fixed referent. Labor time has ceased to count as the absolute touchstone.

Under aleatory conditions, arbitrariness becomes the law: lies, violence, and corruption are no longer marginal offshoots of economic life, but tend to become the alpha and omega of the daily management of affairs. Bands of criminals decisively take command. Economic power belongs to those who possess more powerful language machines. The governance of the mediascape, dominance in the production of software, and control over financial information: these are the foundations of economic power. And the domination of these sources of power cannot be established by means of the dear old competition, through which the best possible management of available resources wins, but rather through lies, deceit, and war. There is no longer any economic power that is not criminal, that does not violate fundamental human rights: first and foremost the right to education, self-knowledge, and the right to a nonpolluted infosphere.

THE ITALIAN ANOMALY

Providing a definition of the regime that was established in Italy in 1994—the year of the first victory of Forza Italia (the TV-football Party)—is more than a question of naming. Like other periods in the history of Italy in the twentieth century, the years of Berlusconi are indicative of an Italian anomaly, and functioned as a laboratory for experimentation with social trends. Other historical moments when Italy was the laboratory of new tendencies were 1922, when techniques of populist and totalitarian management were experimented with in the name of Fascism, and the 1970s.

In the 1970s, an anomalous though exemplary situation arose: the students' movement of 1968 gave rise to a long period of social insubordination and autonomy from work that changed the whole of society. Power responded to this social autonomy by developing an authoritarian and closed system founded on an alliance between the main churches in the country: Catholicism and Stalinism. This was the period of the "historic compromise" and the judicial repression of dissent. The political constriction of this regime and the repression of grassroots movements resulted in a strengthening of armed factions, which led to a wave of terrorism that culminated in the kidnapping and killing of Aldo Moro. But what is the Italian anomaly today, and in what sense is Italy a laboratory of new forms of power? Are we confronted with a reinstatement of Mussolini's regime, as many events in Italian politics seem to suggest?

The answer is no: this is not a fascist regime. This regime is not founded on the repression of dissent; nor does it rest on the enforcement of silence. On the contrary, it relies on the proliferation of chatter, the irrelevance of opinion and discourse, and on making thought, dissent, and critique banal and ridiculous. Even though there have been and will continue to be instances of censorship and direct repression of critical and free thought, these phenomena are rather marginal when compared to what is essentially an immense informational overload and an actual siege of attention, combined with the occupation of the sources of information by the head of the company.

The present social composition cannot be equated with that of Italy in the 1920s, which was predominantly comprised of peasantry and country folk. In the first decades of the twentieth century, the Futurist modernism of Fascism introduced an element of innovation and social progress, whereas today the regime of Forza Italia carries no germ of progress, and its political economy is based on the decay of every legacy of the past. While Fascism initiated a process of productive modernization in the country, the regime of Forza Italia wasted the resources accumulated over years of industrial development, much as Carlos Menem did in Argentina during the decade preceding the collapse of the Argentine economy and society. This drive to dissipation and waste is in perfect harmony with the main global tendency in the period of neoliberal unpredictability.

To understand the specific character of the Italian situation of the past fourteen years, we need to look for what differentiated it from the rest of Europe throughout modernity. We should also consider the postmodern peculiarity of the Italian transformation in the wider context of changes throughout the global system of production and the planetary infosphere. To grasp this specificity we should begin with the Counter-Reformation, which sanctioned the differential speeds of the advancement of the Christian world toward the colonization of the Earth and the construction of modern bourgeois capitalism. The temporality of the countries permeated by the Counter-Reformation (Italy, Spain, Austria, and Poland) is different from that of Protestant countries.

According to Max Weber, classical industrial development is sustained by the Protestant mentality. After the Protestant Reformation, the European bourgeoisie was able to build the foundations of its power by subjecting itself to a rigid ethical and existential discipline. The bourgeois assumes responsibility for her actions and is accountable for them before men and God—but most of all before the bank manager. Economic fortune is a worldly confirmation of divine benevolence.

In contrast, after the Council of Trent (1545–63), the Catholic Counter-Reformation reinstated the primacy of the religious over the secular realm, and defended the conviction that respecting the ecclesiastic hierarchy is much more important than productive discipline. The deep substratum of Catholic culture resists productivity and bourgeois efficiency. If Calvinism was based on the observance of the law, then the spirit of the Counter-Reformation reinforced the primacy of mercy and the absolute value of repentance. The Counter-Reformation remained deeply ingrained in the Italian social imaginary throughout modernity and manifested itself in all its reactionary force at decisive moments in the life of the country. During the Neapolitan revolution of 1799, the enlightened bourgeoisie was isolated and defeated thanks to the complicity of the people with the power of the House of Bourbon, the Church's ally. From the 1800s onwards, the alliance of the Church with the rural classes acted as an antibourgeois conservative force in the defense of the cultural hegemony of the Church against all attempts at secularization of national life. In the years that followed the Second World War, Christian Democracy was the dominant political force, representing the mediation in a permanent equilibrium between capitalist modernization and populist and reactionary resistance. However, it would be wrong to see the "laxness" that derives from the spirit of the Counter-Reformation as a purely regressive and conservative energy.

In the 1970s, the "Italian anomaly" was the expression used to underline the peculiarity of a country where the social movements, which elsewhere had been exhausted in 1968, continued to dominate the political scene for over a decade. In the 1970s, the workers' resistance produced structures of mass organization and fuelled revolts against capitalist modernization. At the time, the Italian anomaly consisted in the persistence of workers' autonomy and social conflict. Italy underwent a long season of proletarian struggles that embraced antimodernism in a dynamic and paradoxically progressive way.

This process began in July 1960, when workers in many cities rose up against the attempt to form a center-right government that included men linked to the old Fascist regime, and culminated in the anti-authoritarian and libertarian insurrection of 1977. Throughout the autonomous workers' struggles against the patronage of the government in cities and factories, we find a constant element: the refusal to subordinate life to work. This refusal was manifest in many of different ways: first of all as Mediterranean idleness, the privileging of sensuality and solar life over productivity and the economy. Then it was expressed in revolts by youths and workers against the rhythms of the factory, and in endemic absenteeism and workers' disaffection with their labor. The movement of workers' autonomy that flourished from 1967 to 1977 sums up this attitude of insubordination and resistance in the idea of the "refusal of work."

The notion of the refusal of work, as it was adopted in Italy during the 1970s, was inserted in the framework of a progressive political strategy. Workers refused the effort and repetitiveness of mechanical labor, thus forcing companies to keep restructuring. Workers' resistance was an element of human progress and freedom, as well as an accelerator of technological and organizational development.

SHIRKERS

At the origin of the mass refusal of productive discipline lies an anti-Calvinist culture. Contrary to the Protestant idea of progress as founded on work discipline, the autonomous, antiwork spirit claims that progress—be it technological, cultural or social—is based on the refusal of discipline. Progress consists of the application of intelligence to the reduction of effort and dependency, and the expansion of a sphere of idleness and individual freedom.

The technological, social, and cultural progress of the country was stimulated by this refusal of work. Between the 1960s and 1970s, Italian civil society experienced its only authentically democratic period, an extraordinary flourishing of culture that coincided with the refusal of work at its most intense and a heightened level of absenteeism in the factories.

Obviously, the refusal of capitalist exploitation, the opposition to increases in productivity and to workers' subordination were not peculiar to Italy. All around the world, workers demanded more free time for their lives, wage increases, and opposed the masters' will to subordinate life to work and work to profit. However, in Italy, this insubordination joined the shirkers' spirit of the southern plebs to become an explicit, declared, and politically relevant issue: that is, the refusal of work and the demand for social autonomy, the autonomy of everyday life from work discipline.

Toward the end of the 1970s, tens of thousands of young southerners arrived at the Fiat factory, Mirafiori. With their new forms of struggle and antiwork attitude, they carried an extremism that was dangerous to both the progressive bourgeoisie and the Italian Communist Party. This new influx of workers completely ignored, if not derided, the work ethic and pride in productivity.

Did these young workers from Naples and Calabria embody the same rascal spirit, the individualist and antimodernist populism, that characterized 1799 and led the Neapolitan people to oppose the enlightened revolutionary bourgeoisie? Yes, in part. But this shirkers' spirit also expressed the new realization that the society of industrial labor was nearing its end. This idea spread through youth culture and invaded the whole of society: industrial labor was a remnant of the past, the development of technologies and social knowledge opened up the possibility for the liberation of society from labor. The most radical parts of the workers' movement expressed the belief that industrial labor was exhausted, and that alienating and repetitive work was therefore no longer historically justified. This idea was the most radical innovation of the Italian workers' movement of the 1960s and 1970s, differentiating it from the communist tradition of the 1900s.

Throughout the modernization of the twentieth century, the Italian Left was pushed in two opposite directions. On the one hand, a Protestant, industrialist and modernist soul motivated its protests against social backwardness and demands for better performance and efficiency in the system of production, at the cost of increasing workers' exploitation and subscribing to liberal policies. On the other hand, an antiproductivist, egalitarian, and communitarian soul drove the Left to demonize capitalism and take refuge in forms of a welfare state that helped create parasitical political clienteles. The workers' autonomy of the 1960s and 1970s wedged itself between these two souls of the traditional Left: in its shirkers' form, it embodied an antiproductivism inscribed in Italian culture, but it also anticipated the creative potential that would take center stage in postmodern and postindustrial production.

Workers' autonomy was defeated by police repression, and the capitalist offensive of the early 1980s hit the factory working class with waves of redundancies, paving the way for neoliberal ideology. But Italian-style liberalism cannot be assimilated to the Protestant liberal-bourgeois tradition that flourished in Europe during modernity.

Liberal culture never affirmed itself in Italy as a majoritarian culture of government. During the nineteenth century, the Liberal Party led the *Risorgimento*, but never actually became the majoritarian culture of the Italian bourgeoisie. The compromise of State and Church, and the alliance between the industrial bourgeoisie and reactionary landowners dominated Italian politics in the nineteenth and twentieth centuries. Liberal culture, a component of political Protestantism, always demanded a secular state, yet it remained a minority. In the early 1900s, Piero Gobetti, a liberal, recognized that the only way to free the Italian state from the reactionary influence of Catholicism was through an alliance between liberals and the workers' movement. That alliance was, unfortunately, never realized, and Fascism destroyed both the communist workers' movement led by Antonio Gramsci and the liberal movement represented by Gobetti. Neoliberalism, as a hegemonic political force, affirmed itself in the 1980s and has nothing to do with the liberal legacy; in fact, it proposes an alliance between all socially and culturally reactionary forces under the banner of ultracapitalist economic "liberalism" in the Anglo-American sense.

In the 1980s, amidst a capitalist counteroffensive and the international affirmation of neoliberalism, Italy gave life to a curious experiment in political economy. After defeating workers' autonomy, social radicalism, and egalitarian and libertarian movements, an anti-Protestant ethic permitted the political class in government to tolerate economic illegalities, embezzlements, corruption, and mafia. These were the years of Bettino Craxi. Despite his socialist and secular credentials, Craxi was the representative of a convergence of the Counter-Reformation spirit of tolerance and shirking, and a cultural openness toward neoliberal modernization. Modernization and corruption, in Craxi's theory and praxis, were not in contradiction; these trends were absolutely complementary, integrated, and functional.

In the 1970s, the historic Left (Communist Party and Catholic Left) responded with violence to the anti-Protestant refusal of work of the youth and workers. They accused the antiwork rebels of the factories and the "Metropolitan Indians" of the social centers of hooliganism. In the 1980s, Catholics and former Communists rebelled against Craxi, not because he was pursuing a neoliberal policy of patronage, but because he tolerated corruption.

Bettino Craxi had sensed what was to come with the affirmation of the neoliberal doctrine. In the 1980s and 1990s, as neoliberalism wrote off all the old regulations of the welfare state, the defenses society had built against the aggressiveness of capitalists collapsed. Craxi understood, with laic cynicism, that neoliberalism inaugurated a period in which the laws of violence, mafia, fraud, corruption and simulation would be the only rules of the game. Catho-communism, in its agony, desperately clung onto the ethical question. Instead of opposing neoliberalism—which destroys society's defenses, reduces workers' wages, imposes a culture of competitiveness and bargaining—the Left opposed corruption, immorality, and illegality. Paradoxically, the Left defended the Protestant ethics that were being dissolved in the culture of big capital, as the traditional bourgeoisie was disappearing to make room for a class of *lumpen* predators.

ALEATORY VALUE IN NEO-BAROQUE SOCIETY

For a long time, the crisis of the law of value has been corroding the foundation of bourgeois society: the bourgeoisie lost its coherence due to the development of postmechanical technologies and the growing autonomy of workers from wage labor. In the postindustrial economy, socially necessary labor time no longer determines value, is no longer its only source. The value of a commodity is essentially determined by means of language, and the regime for determining the value of commodities is one of simulation. The explosion of the *new economy* in the 1990s was the perfect example of the economic power of simulation. Imaginary flows of capital were invested in the production of the imaginary. This does not mean, however, that it was all a blinding illusion.

We have entered the regime of the chance fluctuation of values. The mathematical regularity of bookkeeping has given place to the indeterminacy of financial games and advertising communication, with its linguistic strategies and psychic implications. The economy has become an essentially semiotic process and embodies the chance that characterizes the processes through which meaning is assigned.

Labor has become fractalized. With the end of large industrial monopolies, new workers, now delocalized in the global peripheries, start resembling computer terminals, cells in the circulation of the commodity-sign. As the neat borders of industrial society faded out and broke down in atomized workplaces, *net slaves* underwent two parallel processes. On the one hand, their existence was individualized, both physically and culturally. Each one had to follow her trajectory and compete in the market individually. On the other hand, each worker experienced a situation of permanent cellular connection. Each individual is a cell put in constant productive connection with others by the Web, which ensures a deterritorialized, fractal, and fluid sociality. The cellular is the new assembly line, deprived of any carnal sociality.

Simulation and fractalization are essentially Baroque categories. In the shift to postmodernity, the rationalist balance of industrial architecture gave way to the proliferation of points of view. In *L'età neobarocca* [*The Neo-Baroque Era*] Omar Calabrese (1987) claims that the postmodern style recuperated aesthetic and discursive models that were experimented with in the 1600s. The Baroque was essentially a proliferation of points of view. While Protestant rigor produces an aesthetic of essential and austere images, the Baroque declares the divine generation of forms to be irreducible to human laws, be they of the state, politics, accounting, or architecture.

As Deleuze (1993) claims, the Baroque is the fold: the poetics that best corresponds to the chance character of fluctuating values. When the grand narratives of modernity lose coherence, the law of value is dissolved in an endless proliferation of productivity, inflation, and language, and the infosphere is expanded beyond measure. Mythologies intertwine in the social imaginary. Production and semiosis are increasingly one and the same process. Out of this process simultaneously arise a crisis of economic reference (the relationship between value and necessary labor time) and a crisis of semiotic reference (the denotative relationship between sign and meaning). Value can no longer refer to labor time, because unlike the labor of Marx's era, the duration of immaterial labor is not reducible to an average social norm. Parallel to this, the denotative relation of sign and meaning is definitely suspended in social communication. Advertising, politics, and the media speak a self-declared simulative language. Nobody believes in the truth of public statements. The value of the commodity is established on the basis of a simulation in a relation that no longer follows any rules.

Silvio Berlusconi's behavior is incomprehensible to the conservative Right and Left, whose political logic follows traditional models. They see respect for official language as indispensable, and cannot imagine a context for political action outside adherence to the law. But the strength of Berlusconi's media-populism lies precisely in the systematic violation of taboos linked to political officialdom and legality. With their glum seriousness, authoritative figures like Oscar Luigi Scalfaro and Carlo Azeglio Ciampi are good examples of how the new character of postpolitical language championed by Berlusconi is misunderstood. What seems most unbearable and provocative to the custodians of severity is Berlusconi's sly and systematic ridiculing of political rhetoric and its stagnant rituals. But there is reason to believe that the vast majority of people who constitute the "public" of politics (the electorate) were amused by this ridiculing and provocative gesture, and in many cases won over by it: they identified with the slightly crazy Premier, the rascal Prime Minister who resembles them, in the same way that, at other times, they had identified with Mussolini and Craxi.

The majority of the Italian electorate grew up as TV audiences at a time when television became the primary vehicle for informality, vulgar and coarse allusiveness, the language of ambiguity and aggressiveness. Thus, they spontaneously found themselves on the same cultural wavelength as Berlusconi, with his language, words, and gestures, but also with the deprecation of rules in the name of a spontaneous energy that rules can no longer bridle. The crazy and cheerful figure of Ubu Roi is irresistible to a public that is used to renouncing its individuality in the name of collective irresponsibility.

To the plebeian coarseness of Berlusconi and his perky banqueters in government, the Left responded with prissiness and consternation in the face of the violation of the language of political correctness. But shouting "Scandal!" proved to be a losing argument against the policies of the center-right government. In fact, part of the secret of Berlusconi's success in politics lies precisely in the use of excess. The excessiveness of the declarations and actions of this government was a winner in electoral decisions, and in the imaginary of the masses. Events that exceeded the framework of predictability, tolerability, and codified political behavior acted as catalysts for consternation, and indignation, while easing the way for government legislation, dilapidation of collective property, abolition of workers' rights, and imposition of discriminatory and racist laws. This technique of excess is now well tested: you have to talk big, very big, in order to then enact what is essential for the accumulation of power and the privatization of social spaces. A minister would take on the role of the ham, the lunatic, and propose to bomb the ships carrying migrants to Italian shores. He generates scandal, but also an entertaining distraction, and soon enough another minister, more moderate and realistic, demands military control of the coast, and then a zealous functionary can expel Kurdish and Syrian political asylum seekers without even looking at their requests or knowing their rights. This is how trampling on the most basic rights of foreign workers becomes possible.

Berlusconi's language appears to be suited to ridicule rather than to the denial or restatement of the truth and the affirmation of new principles. His intention is to unveil the hypocrisy of political rules. For Berlusconi, the meaning of words is unimportant, so unimportant that he is used to denying his own declarations in newspapers the day after making them. Berlusconi often pretends to approve of the words of the President of the Republic, even when these words blatantly contravene his own actions or the legislative activities of his government. The political word is devalued, ridiculed, captured in a kind of three-card monty, in a semantic labyrinth where every word can mean the opposite of the meaning attributed to it in dictionaries. Being scandalized by the informality, vulgarity, and shallow lies is not an effective reaction; on the contrary it strengthens Berlusconi and his regime because, at this level, the electorate understands him better than the representatives of mundane government.

According to common sense, political language has always concealed reality and provided hypocritical cover-ups to the arbitrariness and arrogance of the rich and powerful. Berlusconi paradoxically reveals this hypocrisy. He is the rich and powerful one who shows that the law is capable of nothing; he is the rich and powerful one who laughs at the hypocrisy of those who pretend that everyone is equal before the law. We all know that everyone is not equal before the law;

we know from experience that the wealthy and powerful can afford expensive lawyers, impose their interests, and conquer spaces in power inaccessible to the majority of the population. But this is usually hidden behind the smoke screens of legalism and juridical formalism. Berlusconi clearly states: "I do what I want, and laugh at the legalists who want to oppose their formalities to my will."

Now that the power of making and unmaking the law lies in his hands, he uses it to show everyone the impotence of the law. Like Humpty Dumpty, Berlusconi knows that what matters is not what words mean, but who owns them. Meaning is decided by the master of words, not the semantic tribunals. The interpretation of law is decided by its master, not the courts of law.

The spectators of politics (the electorate) seem to recognize themselves in this game of revealing the hypocrisy of political language, even though the person revealing that the "Emperor has no clothes" is paradoxically wearing the Emperor's clothes. People laugh at what the Travicello King says, but there is complicity in their laughter, because the King is denouncing the falsity and hypocrisy of the words he himself is uttering, with a smile that says: "Here, I say it and deny it," or "There are no fools here."[2]

The boring opponents of Berlusconi want to reaffirm the sacredness of power, but Berlusconi has already discredited it with his exercise of a power that has no need for sacredness. Despite being divested of official authority, the Berlusconi government enjoys the authoritativeness of transgression; it exercises its authority in the name of transgression, laying down laws on every issue, from immigration to the right to work and the judiciary, imposing everywhere the logic of hegemonic interests, reducing social expenditure, shifting wealth from the working classes to the property owners. None of the devastating laws of this government were stopped by parliamentary opposition or the protests of democratic and priggish public opinion.

---

2   A "Travicello" is a small piece of wood that might be carried away by the floods of a river. In this context, it suggests someone volatile, futile, and frivolous. The "Travicello King" is a character described by the Italian poet Giuseppe Giusti (one of the most renowned poets of Italian Risorgimento), referring to Carlo Alberto, the irresolute King of the Regno di Savoia in 1848.

SELF DESPISE

Have we come close to a definition of the regime that has governed Italy since 1994? I believe so. This regime includes the behaviors of Fascism (police brutality, as we saw in Genoa 2001, the irresponsibility that led Mussolini's Italy to the catastrophic war of 1940–45, the servility that has always characterized Italian intellectual life). It also includes features that are proper to the mafia (the contempt for the public good, the toleration of economic lawlessness).

But it cannot be defined as a mere repetition of the Fascist regime, nor as a mafia system. Aggressive neoliberalism and media-populism are its decisive features. It objectively functions as a laboratory for the cultural and political forms crucial to the development of semiocapital.

The history of modern Italy ought to be written taking the farcical proclamations of the Risorgimento, Fascism, and the democratic republic less seriously. A history could be written starting from the work of Lorenzo Valla, his elegy of vileness and hedonism, and Niccolò Machiavelli, with his affirmation of the incompatibility of morality and politics. It could be centered around Manzoni's don Abbondio, and around the characters Vittorio Gassman and Alberto Sordi play in the film *The Great War,* roles that embody the popular wisdom that always refuses to believe that one's country is more important than one's life. And it should take into account the Mediterranean cult of femininity, hedonism and tenderness.

The refusal of Protestant austerity and self-sacrifice is the essence of the Italian adventure, the elasticity and intelligence of a people who never believed in the mother country or the general interest and who, because of this, can't be reduced to the logic of capitalism that identifies the general interest with profit and growth.

This refusal lacked the courage of its convictions, and remained a marginal prerogative of the lower classes, excluded from history. Official language identified with rhetoric reminiscent of Roman empires, thus creating the conditions, on the one hand, for the self-deprecation that rules over Italian public discourse and, on the other, the pompous and empty affirmation of Italian nationalism and the Fascism that is its natural expression. The main thread in the history of this country and the self-perception of the Italian people is a mixture of unavowed cowardice and self-contempt, the source of the aggressiveness that finds its full expression in Fascism. The Latin cult of virility that aggressively posits itself above the tenderness and femininity of Mediterranean culture is both tragic and farcical.

Cowardice is ambivalent: in its immediacy, it signals the hedonist consciousness of the supremacy of pleasure over historical duty. But this consciousness does not reconcile with the imperialist and macho mythologies embodied in the tragic farce of Fascism. Unable to accept cowardice as tenderness, unable to accept the predominance of the feminine in Mediterranean culture, Italian history is full of farcical characters who take on heroic tasks and inevitably cause tragedies, the ridiculous implications of which can never be concealed. The figure of Salandra, who starts crying during the Versailles Congress because the British would not listen to Italian demands, finds its counterpart in the figure of Mussolini, who wants to vindicate the "mutilated victory" of the First World War and exalts the masculine masses with the promise of reckless military adventures, eventually leading the country to a catastrophic war.

By comparing its present hedonism and subaltern status to a mythological past of imperial superiority, Italian culture revels in self-contempt, because it refuses to accept its feminine side. When it tried to react to self-contempt by affirming an improbable virility, it embarked on infamous and truly paltry adventures, such as the vile attack on France after it had already been defeated by Hitler in the late spring of 1940, or in its habit of running to help the winners only to discover that, with its help, they end up losing.

There are rare moments when self-contempt turns into a positive valorization of tenderness, abandonment, and idleness: these are the only times when Italian culture produced something original, when Mediterranean femininity was placated in the collective enjoyment of the potentialities developed by the collective productive intelligence. In the 1960s and 1970s the predominant movement in society veered toward abandoning all imperialist pretenses and embracing a joyous quality of life, freed from the urgency of economic productivity.

The movement in Italy can start again from a declaration of absolute weakness, abandonment, and retreat. Let's withdraw our intelligence from the race of capitalist growth and national identity, let's withdraw our creativity and our time from productive competition. Let's inaugurate a period of passive sabotage and definitively evacuate the ridiculous space of Italian national identity.

chapter four

EXHAUSTION

AND

SUBJECTIVITY

AFTER 2-15-2003

when millions of people marched worldwide against the second US invasion of Iraq, the peace movement lost its strength, and so did the global movement against the corporations.

The social forces that merged in the counterglobalization movement have dispersed, the world landscape has been submerged by the endless war started by Bush and Cheney, and despair has taken a central place in the cultural scene. For three years after the Seattle events of November 1999, the counterglobalization movement organized demonstrations and media-actions all around the globe, but this wave of mobilization never went beyond ethical declarations; it never became a process of social autonomy. During those years, every Saturday afternoon the streets were full of people protesting against this and against that, but on Monday morning the same people were sitting in the offices and factories and schools and laboratories, bending to corporate rule.

After February 15, 2003, impotence prevailed, energy dissolved, and people were forced to accept the blackmail of war, competition, and precarity. But the crucial question is why the social class of the general intellect, the precarious cognitariat and the forces of labor in general, have not been able to create their space of autonomy. In order to understand labor's inability to react to growing exploitation, we have to analyze the effects of recombinant semiocapitalism, and the effects of the precarization of labor.

This is what I want to do in this last part of the book: I want to understand the social and cultural roots of the present palsy of the social organism, overcoming the bitterness that originates from the current humiliation of human life and intelligence. The task of a thinker—assuming that thinking has a task—is not to breathe hope into hearts, but to help in understanding reality, because only understanding can call forth new possibilities.

After a general analysis of the precarization of labor and its effects, I'll plunge into the new landscape that has emerged from the crisis of the global economy. I'll try to describe the evolution of capitalism following the financial catastrophe of September 2008. Furthermore, I'll attempt to describe the relationship between language, affection and sociability in order to look into the future of subjectivation, or lack of it. Finally, I'll explore new theoretical pathways in the field of the imagination of the future.

The outcome of the catastrophe that the financial crisis has triggered, along with the military defeat of the West in Iraq and Afghanistan, is not predictable at the moment. The next decade will be marked by a massive redistribution of power and wealth. But it's impossible to say now if neoliberal ideology will fade, and give way to a return of social solidarity, or if the criminal class that has grown up in the shadow of neoliberal deregulation will instigate ethnic and national war, launching a planetary genocide for the possession of decreasing resources.

So far, the second scenario has been prevailing. In the first year after the financial collapse of September 2008, nation-states have invested a huge amount of money to rescue the financial class that has redirected monetary resources from social needs. The entire society, especially the new generation, has been called upon to pay to save the criminal class. If workers do not find the means to change direction, we are heading toward a growing destruction of the material and immaterial structures of civilized life, a barbarization of the social landscape.

PRECARIOUS FUTURE

The concepts of the subject and subjectivity have been crucial in the philosophy of the last fifty years, from the Hegelian Renaissance of the 1960s, tied to the surfacing of dissent in the socialist countries and anticonsumerist movements in the West, to the neo-Marxist thought of the Italian workerist school, the poststructuralist thought of Deleuze and Guattari, and the genealogical work of Michel Foucault. In the word "subject," two different concepts are contained: one is action, the other is consciousness. Only by grasping the inner mediation that connects the concept of the subject to the idealistic vision of History as the realization of Spirit and Substance, can we understand the complicated evolutions of the subject in modern philosophy. "In my view ... everything turns on grasping and expressing the True, not only as *Substance*, but equally as *Subject*," writes Hegel (1977, 9–10) in the "Preface" to *Phenomenology of Spirit*. He also argues that: "The living Substance is being which is in truth *Subject*, or, what is the same, is in truth actual only in so far as it is the movement of positing itself, or is the mediation of its self-othering with the self" (10). And finally: "The True is the whole. But the whole is nothing other than the essence consummating itself through its development. Of the Absolute it must be said that it is essentially a *result*, that only in the *end* is it what it truly is; and that precisely in this consists its nature, viz. to be actual, subject, the spontaneous becoming of itself" (11).

Consciousness is implied in the Hegelian concept of the subject, because consciousness is the mediation between the action and its actor. But here I want to elaborate precisely on the relationship between action and consciousness, as I am questioning the conscious character of social action in the recombinant age. Therefore, here I dismiss the concept of the "subject" (as it implies consciousness) and substitute the word "actor."

I speak of agency, of a collective actor, of singularity in the Guattarian sense, and, finally, I speak of "movement." Movement is the process of society: the cultural process that makes possible the political unity of different social actors who are in conflict in public space. When social actors find a common ground of understanding and act together for a common goal, I see a movement, the active and conscious side of social transformation, and also of cultural evolution. Movement is the subjective (conscious and collective) aspect of the recomposition of the living social sphere against the domination of the dead (capital).

At the end of the zero zero decade, for the first time in my life, I've been obliged to recognize that the actor is absent: you see actions, but you don't see an actor. Actions without an actor play out on the ground of social visibility, but they don't create any common ground in the space of consciousness and affectivity. Actions are performed in the theater of social production, but the agent of recombination is not there, in the theater, but backstage, and the consciousness of the process does not belong to the process itself.

Human beings perform productive actions, but they are not conscious actors of what they are doing, and seem unable to unite feeling and thought in a common space of consciousness. Capitalism has destroyed the conditions of recomposition, and society has become unrecomposable. The noncomposability of society means that the process of subjectivation cannot take place. This is why the future has lost its zest and people have lost all trust in it: the future no longer appears as a choice or a collective conscious action, but is a kind of unavoidable catastrophe that we cannot oppose in any way.

The future is the subject of this book: I have tried to rethink what the imagination of the future was during the century marked by the struggles of labor against capitalist exploitation, and by the creation of broad social realms of autonomy from capitalist rule. But for the remainder of the book I'm trying to investigate the present collapse of the imagination of the future, from the point of view of the (apparently) impossible recomposition of social subjectivity. Of course I don't want to stop here, I don't want to be the gloomy doomsayer. But I think that we have to be able to see things as they are, if we want to find a way beyond the present depressing reality.

My point of view has been shaped by two centuries of progressive enlightened history: it is the point of view of an epoch, of a generation that has been always convinced it bears the fulfillment of the modern promise. But this means I have a problem of imagination where the past and future are concerned. The way I imagine and narrate time is connected to the way history has developed during the last two centuries. But the digital mutation, coupled with neoliberal ideology, has completely reframed the perception of time, and the relationship between human beings and their social environment. We can no longer think the flow of collective time within a frame of progressive becoming.

Of course, I see very well that the progressive process has come to a halt in the age of capitalist counteroffensive and media colonization; but, I can't help perceiving this as a temporary halt; I can't stop thinking that my political and cultural energies have to be dedicated entirely to bringing back the old progressive rhythm of history, restoring the order of civilization that I considered eternal during the years of my cultural formation. This attitude is blinding and misleading me, and it's preventing me from understanding what is really going on in the deep structure of the social imagination.

The progressive perception of historical time is a prejudice, and this prejudice puts me on the wrong path, giving me the false impression that something can be done in order to go back to the past history of civilization. On the contrary, nothing can be done, because the periodization I have in mind has to be reframed. Progressive ideology was based on the idealistic premise that the history of mankind is essentially the history of the progressive realization of Reason. Now we are facing a reality that has nothing to do with the realization of Reason, and also has nothing to do with an evolutionary progressive vision. Evolution is not progressive.

The progressive vision is based on the idea that evolution is human-oriented. Evolution is not human-oriented. Evolution has gone beyond the limits of a human-oriented civilization, because the limits of what humans can know or control have been surpassed.

Let us focus on two concepts recently introduced into the debate on labor and subjectivation. The concept of "recomposition" comes from the theoretical laboratory of Italian operaismo. The concept of "recombination" has been proposed by Arthur Kroker and Michael Weinstein (1993) and by the Critical Art Ensemble (1994) in order to define the epistemology of the new technologies (namely informatics and biotech). I want to apply these concepts to the organization of labor in the age of networked globalization.

I define *recombination* as the technical form of the labor process in the digital environment, while *recomposition* means the social and cultural process enabling fragments of labor to become conscious subjectivity. My central thesis is the following: the recombinant form of the labor process has changed the very foundation of exploitation, and has displaced the social landscape in such a way that any social conscious recomposition seems impossible.

We can start with the political side of the problem. For the last two decades, the defeat of the Left around the world has often been explained by the crumbling of socialist states and the subsequent dissolution of the Communist parties. But I think the reasons for the social and political defeat have to be found in the change in labor organization and the cultural mutation produced by the media colonization of the social mind. In recent decades, the fragmentation of the political Left has been a problem, perhaps, and the defeat of the leftist parties in national elections in Europe is a symptom of this crisis. But I think that the basic problem for the progressive movement is the cultural inability to start the process of labor's social recomposition.

Social composition is the cultural process that unifies the social body through the fusion of imaginary and cultural flows. The concept of composition originally comes from chemical science, not from the political lexicon. In the process of social composition, it's possible to find the material genesis of solidarity, or lack of it. The concept of composition has been elaborated in the neo-Marxist Italian theoretical landscape of the 1960s and 1970s (Tronti, Bologna, Negri), in opposition to the dogmatic vision of the prevailing Hegelian historicism of the Italian Communist Party.

In the parlance of the Italian workerist school, the root of the working class's autonomy, its ability to organize against exploitation, is to be found in the fusion of the cultural components of the social fabric. Myth, ideology, media, advertising; these forces are producing effects in the composition of society. They can produce effects of recomposition, when the different segments of social labor find a common ground of sensibility and understanding, and stand united against the exploiters. They can produce effects of decomposition, when technological and ideological capitalist action destroy feelings of friendship, the institutions of labor organization, and society's sympathy for itself.

During the decades of the 1960s and 1970s, world society underwent a process of internal recomposition that made possible the autonomy of the workers' movement from the domination of capital. Then, after the victory of Thatcher and Reagan, capital's counteroffensive smashed the organized force of labor, decentralized the factories, invaded the social brain with corporate media flows, and finally reduced the international cycle of labor to an infinite ocean of microfragments of nervous connection.

The notion of composition is very close to the Guattarian concept of subjectivation. In his books, Guattari says that we should not speak of a subject, in the old Hegelo-dialectical way. The subject is not there from the beginning, as an ideal force, able to fight and win. There are no subjects in history, there are women and men, poor, frail organisms trying to escape misery and death. There are conscious and sensitive organisms expressing desire and creating rhizomes. The social molecules may find common understanding and common sensibility and may act like a subject, if they are able to share the same "refrain," as Guattari would say.

Precarity refers not only to the deregulation of the labor market and the fragmentation of work, but also the dissolution of community. A continuous flow of infolabor runs in the global network, and it is the general factor of capital valorization, but this flow isn't able to subjectivize, to coagulate in the conscious action of the collective body. This is why the labor force has apparently become unrecomposable. Solidarity between the workers of the world was the main basis of democracy during the past century, and the only guarantee of workers' human rights; it no longer exists, having been destroyed by the new division and fragmentation of recombinant labor.

Migrants, precarious workers, cognitive workers: they share the same condition of weakness, in different degrees. But they are unable to find a common ground of solidarity and struggle. This apparent unrecomposability of labor is the effect of the digitalization of the production process, and of the subsequent fractalization and precarization of labor.

In the global digital network, labor is transformed into small parcels of nervous energy picked up by the recombining machine. In this sense, I would say that it is fractalized, and recombined by the techno-financial network. The workers are deprived of every individual consistency. Strictly speaking, the workers no longer exist. Their time exists, their time is there, permanently available to connect, to produce in exchange for a temporary salary.

Marx's prophecy about the "atom of time" is fulfilled. In the process of networked production we no longer find working persons, but abstract, depersonalized, fractal atoms of time available in the netsphere. This is why the labor force has become unrecomposable, unable to recognize itself as a community of sensible and sensitive beings who share the same social interests and the same cultural expectations.

Is the recomposition process (which we can call a process of collective subjectivation) still possible in this new condition? The productive force of cognitive labor has been multiplied by the creation of the recombinant network. The "general intellect" to which Marx refers in the *Grundrisse* is the ability of knowledge to act as a value-producing force. Thanks to the introduction of digital machines, capital has incorporated the product of the general brain in its system of machines. But the living process of knowledge still resides in the mind of the individual scientist and technician.

In the digital network we are dealing with a different reality: the living brains of individuals are absorbed (subsumed) inside the process of network production and submitted to a system of technolinguistic automatisms. Recombination is the (informational and biopolitical) technique that transforms the activity of individual brains in an abstract productive continuum. The individual brain can act effectively only through the recombinant modality: functional recombination of fragments of cognitive labor scattered in time and space, but functionally unified inside the Net.

Interoperability is the general goal of the network, and in order to connect, the recombinant fragments of living labor time have to become compatible:

> The core problem of getting computers to communicate with each other is, by definition, one of compatibility. As the network grows bigger, incompatibilities must be overcome ... if an incompatibility emerges, it produces a trigger for change requiring new technical and social negotiations. Generally however a new protocol or level is introduced that, by operating between or on top of different layers, will allow them all to coexist under a single common framework. (Terranova 2004, 58–59).

Desingularization of living thought and activity is mandatory for access to the network. In the global network there are not working persons, but an infinite brain-sprawl, an ever-changing mosaic of fractal cells of available nervous energy. The person is nothing but the residue—therefore precarious—of the process of valorization.

From the point of view of subjectivation, the productive and functional potency of cognitive labor, its interoperability, seems to be inversely proportional to its social and political recomposability. The collective brain is functionally recombined in the sphere of the Net. But at the social and affective level, the social brain appears unable to recompose, to find common strategies of behavior, incapable of common narration and of solidarity. Therefore, the expansion of the productive potency of the general intellect coincides with a schizoid fragmentation of the collective brain, incapable of recomposing as conscious subjectivity, unable to act in a conscious, collective way.

During modernity, the industrial labor force was composed by persons, bearers of individual ability to perform tasks, and also bearers of physical needs and political rights, like the right to unionize, negotiate, and strike. Today, the labor force can be described as a sprawl of nervous energy, of depersonalized time available to cellular recombination. This time has been fractalized and compatibilized and so made recombinable. In order to interoperate, the individual mind has to become a cell of the networked mind, a compatible fractal: this implies a technological mutation but also a psychic mutation of the living mind.

As Christian Marazzi has explained in his books, language and capital tighten their relationship: language becomes the economic resource, the productive force, and the market. This is why I speak of semiocapital: the realm of signs and the realm of production tend to coincide.

Language undergoes a mutation, which is both technological and psychic. In the human psyche, as Freud says, the access to language has much to do with affection and primarily with the body of the mother. What happens to the linguistic relationship between the mother and child when the infosphere is saturated with infostimuli and the mother's presence becomes so scarce? In *The Show and Tell Machine*, published in 1977, the American anthropologist Rose Goldsen argued that we are giving birth to human beings who will learn more words from machines than from mothers. In the first decade of the new century, this generation has occupied the stage of social activity, and is ready to become compatible with the digital flow.

For the new generation, access to language has more and more to do with inorganic connection, and less and less to do with the body of the mother. In her book *L'ordine simbolico della madre* [*The Symbolic Order of the Mother*], Luisa Muraro (1991) explores the intimate relationship between signifier and signified, between sign and meaning, between word and affection. I believe in the meaning of the word "water" and I acknowledge the relationship between the signifier "water" and the liquid because I trust in my mother. She has certified the relation between signifier and signified. What happens when the relation is broken, when access to language is separated from the body and from affection, reduced to mere interoperability between machinic segments of an emotionless exchange? Language is made precarious, frail, unable to grasp the emotional meaning of words. Actually, the generation that is now entering the social sphere seems psychologically frail and scarcely fit to link emotion and verbal exchange. The huge multiplication of tools for communication, the digital saturation of the infosphere, has dramatically reduced the spaces and the times of bodily interaction between persons.

Let us think of the crowd of people sitting in the subway every morning. They are precarious workers moving toward the industrial and financial districts of the city, toward the places where they are working in precarious conditions. Everyone wears headphones, everybody looks at their cellular device, everybody sits alone and silent, never looking at the people who sit close, never speaking or smiling or exchanging any kind of signal. They are traveling alone in their lonely relationship with the universal electronic flow. Their cognitive and affective formation has made of them the perfect object of a process of desingularization. They have been pre-emptied and transformed into carriers of abstract fractal ability to connect, devoid of sensitive empathy so as to become smooth, compatible parts of a system of interoperability. Although they suffer from nervous aggression, and from the exploitation that semiocapitalism is imposing on them, although they suffer from the separation between functional being and sensible body and mind, they seem incapable of human communication and solidarity; in short, they seem unable to start any process of conscious collective subjectivation.

The infosphere is the dimension of intentional signs surrounding the sensible organism. Sensibility is an interface between organism and world: we might see it specifically as the ability to understand the meaning of what cannot be said through words, the point of connection between sensitivity and language. Sensibility rather than judgment is where the mental mutation produced by the infosphere happens. Changes of perception are intertwined with the technological architecture surrounding the perceptive organism. Prior to modernity, a regime of slow transmission characterized the infosphere, man's psychic time, and his expectations of events and signals. The acceleration of semiotic transmission and the proliferation of sources of information transformed the perception of living time. The infosphere became more rapid and dense, and sensibility underwent increasing exposure to the flow of infostimuli. Due to an intensification of electronic signals, sensibility was dragged into a vertigo of simulated stimulation that increased its speed to panic levels.

The perception of the other and its body is reshaped, too. Pressure, acceleration, and automation affect gestural, postural behavior and the whole disposition and interaction of bodies in space. At the foundation of social concern with spatial arrangements lies an effort to elaborate, hide, excite, or repress eroticism. The social arrangement of space intervenes to change the disposition of the bodies that meet in the street or sit together in the office or at school. Societies also experience varying degrees of tension and aggressiveness according to the different ways they manage eroticism and the circulation of bodies.

Throughout the history of civilization, perception has been molded by artificial regimes of images and techniques of representation. Through digital technology the image begins to proliferate vertiginously and our faculty of imagination undergoes vortices of acceleration. The image should not be considered as the brute perception of empirical data brought to our visual attention by matter: it is rather the effect of a semiconscious elaboration. The technical mode through which we receive and elaborate images acts upon the formation of the imaginary. The imaginary, in turn, shapes the imagination, the activity whereby we produce images, imagine worlds, and thus make them possible in real life. The repertoire of images at our disposal limits, exalts, amplifies, or circumscribes the forms of life and events that, through our Imagination, we can project onto the world, put into being, build, and inhabit.

Technocommunicative and psychocognitive mutations are as interdependent as the organism and its ecosystem. The conscious organism is also sensuous; it is a bundle of sensitive receptors. The infosphere is more and more transformed into a tv-zapping, nonlinear, and highly chaotic flow. The social unconscious does not easily adapt to this transformation of the infosphere, because the social investment of desire is structured around the nucleus of identity, which is fleeing and dissolving in all directions.

Suddenly awoken by this semiotic proliferation, deprived of the filters that the critical and disciplinary mind of modernity once possessed, the conscious organism reacts with panic. The communicative power of digital technology produces an excess of information with respect to the socially available time of attention. How is sensibility redefined and how does it adapt to over stimulation?

I think that the effect of semiocapitalist acceleration and overexploitation of nervous energies is exhaustion. Nervous breakdown, psychopathology, panic, depression, suicidal epidemic. "A titanic battle is about to begin, a Darwinian struggle between competing psychopathies," says Ballard in *Super-Cannes*, his 2000 book about the psychic catastrophe of the virtual class.

EXHAUSTION:
REREADING BAUDRILLARD

The concept of exhaustion entered public discourse in the 1970s with the publication of *Limits to Growth*, a report for the Club of Rome:

> Under the direction of a team of systems analysts based at Massachusetts Institute of Technology ... the report gave voice to the prevailing consensus that Fordist manufacture had entered a period of irreversible decline. But it also brought something palpably new to the analysis. If there was a crisis in the offing, it was not one that could be measured in conventional economic terms—a crisis in productivity or economic growth rates—but rather a wholesale crisis in the realm of reproduction. For the Club of Rome what was at stake was no less than the continuing reproduction of the earth's biosphere and hence the future of life on earth. The most visible signs of the impending crisis were therefore to be found in the existence of all kind of ecological disequilibria, exhaustion, and breakdown, from rising levels of pollution to famine and the increase in extinction rates. (Cooper 2008, 15–16).

The report refers to the physical resources, not to the dangers of overexploitation of the nervous energies of the social mind. But the report wreaked havoc, because for the first time the intrinsic impossibility of unlimited growth was revealed. In her remarkable book, Melinda Cooper relates the concept of exhaustion to the fields of biology and mental energy. Cooper writes:

> Twenty years later, armed with more sophisticated modeling tools, the same team came up with a slightly more nuanced prognosis for the future. Limits to growth, they now argued, were time-like rather than space-like. This meant that we might have already gone beyond the threshold at which an essential resource such as oil could be sustainably consumed, long before we would notice its actual depletion. In fact, it was highly probable according to the report's author, that we were already living beyond our limit, in a state of suspended crisis, innocently waiting for the

future to boomerang back in our faces. Time is in fact the ultimate limit in the world's model. (Cooper 2008, 16–17).

Time is in the mind. The essential limit to growth is the mental impossibility to extend time (cybertime) beyond a certain point. I
think that we are here touching upon a crucial point. The process of
recomposition, of conscious and collective subjectivation, finds here a
new—paradoxical—path. Modern radical thought has always seen subjectivation as an energetic process: mobilization, social desire and political activism, expression, participation have been the modes of conscious
collective subjectivation in the age of the revolutions. But in our age, energy is running out and desire, which has given modern social dynamics
their soul, is absorbed in the black hole of virtualization and financial
games, as Jean Baudrillard argues in his 1976 book, *Symbolic Exchange
and Death*. In this book, Baudrillard analyzes the hyperrealistic stage of
capitalism, and the instauration of the logic of simulation.

> The end of the spectacle brings with it the collapse of reality into
> hyperrealism, the meticulous reduplication of the real, prefera-
> bly through another reproductive medium such as advertising or
> photography. Through reproduction from one medium into an-
> other the real becomes volatile, it becomes the allegory of death,
> but it also draws strength from its own destruction, becoming
> the real for its own sake, a fetishism of the lost object which is no
> longer the object of representation, but the ecstasy of denegation
> and its own ritual extermination: the hyperreal. [...]

> The reality principle corresponds to a certain stage of the law of
> value. Today the whole system is swamped by indeterminacy,
> and every reality is absorbed by the hyperreality of the code and
> simulation. The principle of simulation governs us now, rather
> that the outdated reality principle. We *feed* on those forms whose
> finalities have disappeared. No more ideology, only simulacra.
> We must therefore reconstruct the entire genealogy of the law
> of value and its simulacra in order to grasp the hegemony and
> the enchantment of the current system. A structural revolution
> of value. This genealogy must cover political economy, where it
> will appear as a second-order simulacrum, just like all those that

stake everything on the real: the real of production, the real of signification, whether conscious or unconscious.

Capital no longer belongs to the order of political economy: it operates with political economy as its simulated model. The entire apparatus of the commodity law of value is absorbed and recycled in the larger apparatus of the structural law of value, this becoming part of the third order of simulacra. Political economy is thus assured a *second life*, an eternity, within the confines of an apparatus in which it has lost all its strict determinacy, but maintains an effective presence as a system of reference for simulation. (Baudrillard 1993a: 71-72, 2).

Simulation is the new plane of consistency of capitalist growth: financial speculation, for instance, has displaced exploitation from the sphere of material production to the sphere of expectations, desire, and immaterial labor. The simulation process (cyberspace) is proliferating without limits, irradiating signs that go everywhere in the attention market. In semiocapitalist hyperreality, the brain is the market. And the brain is not limitless, the brain cannot expand and accelerate indefinitely.

Collective subjectivation (i.e. social recomposition) implies the development of a common language-affection, which must happen in the temporal dimension. The semiocapitalist acceleration of time has destroyed the social possibility of sensitive elaboration of the semioflow. The proliferation of simulacra in the infosphere has saturated the space of attention and imagination. Advertising and stimulated hyperexpression ("just do it"), have submitted the energies of the social psyche to permanent mobilization. Exhaustion follows, and exhaustion is the only escape:

> Nothing, not even the system, can avoid the symbolic obligation, and it is in this trap that the only chance of a catastrophe for capital remains. The system turns on itself, as a scorpion does when encircled by the challenge of death. For it is summoned to answer, if it is not to lose face, to what can only be death. The system must *itself commit suicide in response to the multiplied challenge of death and suicide.*

So hostages are taken. On the symbolic or sacrificial plane, from which every moral consideration of the innocence of the victims is ruled out, the hostage is the substitute, the alter-ego of the terrorist—the hostage's death for the terrorist's. Hostage and terrorist may thereafter become confused in the same sacrificial act. (Baudrillard 1993a: 37).

In these impressive pages, Baudrillard outlines the end of the modern dialectics of revolution against power, of the labor movement against capitalist domination, and predicts the advent of a new form of action that will be marked by the sacrificial gift of death (and self-annihilation). After the destruction of the World Trade Center in the most important terrorist act ever, Baudrillard wrote a short text titled *The Spirit of Terrorism*, in which he goes back to his own predictions and recognizes the emergence of a catastrophic age. When the code becomes the enemy, the only strategy can be catastrophic:

all the counterphobic ravings about exorcizing evil: it is because it is there, everywhere, like an obscure object of desire. Without this deep-seated complicity, the event would not have had the resonance it has, and in their symbolic strategy the terrorists doubtless know that they can count on this unavowable complicity. (Baudrillard 2003, 6).

This goes much further than hatred for the dominant global power by the disinherited and the exploited, those who fell on the wrong side of global order. This malignant desire is in the very heart of those who share this order's benefits. An allergy to all definitive order, to all definitive power is happily universal, and the two towers of the World Trade Center embodied perfectly, in their very double-ness (literally twin-ness), this definitive order:

No need, then, for a death drive or a destructive instinct, or even for perverse, unintended effects. Very logically—and inexorably—the increase in the power of power heightens the will to destroy it. And it was party to its own destruction. When the two towers collapsed, you had the impression that they were responding to the suicide of the suicide-planes with their own suicides. It has been said that "Even God cannot declare war on Himself." Well, He can. The West, in position of God (divine omnipotence and absolute moral legitimacy), has become suicidal, and declared war on itself. (Baudrillard 2003, 6–7).

In Baudrillard's catastrophic vision I see a new way of thinking subjectivity: a reversal of the energetic subjectivation that animates the revolutionary theories of the twentieth century, and the opening of an implosive theory of subversion, based on depression and exhaustion.

In the activist view, exhaustion is seen as the inability of the social body to escape the vicious destiny that capitalism has prepared: deactivation of the social energies that once upon a time animated democracy and political struggle. But exhaustion could also become the beginning of a slow movement toward a "*wu wei*" civilization, based on the withdrawal, and frugal expectations for life and consumption. Radicalism could abandon the mode of activism, and adopt the mode of passivity. A radical passivity would definitely threaten the ethos of relentless productivity that neoliberal politics has imposed.

The mother of all the bubbles, the work bubble, would finally deflate. We have been working too much during the last three or four centuries, and outrageously too much during the last thirty years. The current depression could be the beginning of a massive abandonment of competition, consumerist drive, and dependence on work. Actually, if we think of the geopolitical struggle of the first decade of the twenty-first century—the struggle between western domination and jihadist Islam—we recognize that the most powerful weapon has been suicide. September 11 was the most impressive act of this suicidal war, but thousands of people have killed themselves in order to destroy American military hegemony. And they've won, forcing the western world into the bunker of paranoid security, defeating the hypertechnological armies of the West both in Iraq, and in Afghanistan.

The suicidal implosion has not been confined to the Islamists. Suicide has became a form of political action everywhere. Against neoliberal politics, Indian farmers have killed themselves. Against exploitation, hundreds of workers and employees have killed themselves in the French factories of Peugeot, and in the offices of France Telecom. In Italy, when the 2009 recession destroyed one million jobs, many workers, haunted by the fear of unemployment, climbed on the roofs of the factories, threatening to kill themselves. Is it possible to divert this implosive trend from the direction of death, murder, and suicide, toward a new kind of autonomy, social creativity and of life?

I think that it is possible only if we start from exhaustion, if we emphasize the creative side of withdrawal. The exchange between life and money could be abandoned, and exhaustion could give way to a huge wave of withdrawal from the sphere of economic exchange. A new refrain could emerge in that moment and wipe out the law of economic growth. The self-organization of the general intellect could abandon the law of accumulation and growth, and start a new concatenation, where collective intelligence is only subjected to the common good.

NECRONOMY

The global recession officially started in September 2008 and officially lasted until the summer of 2009. Since the summer of 2009, the official truth in the media, political statements, and economic talk was *recovery*. Stock market indices began to rise and the banks again started paying huge bonuses to their managers.

Meanwhile, unemployment was exploding everywhere, wages were falling, welfare was curtailed, ninety million more are expected to join the army of poverty in the next year. Is this recovery? Our conditional reflex (influenced by the Keynesian knowledge that recovery is the recovery of the "real economy") answers: no, this is not recovery. Capitalism cannot recover only by financial means.

But we should reframe our vision. Finance is no longer a mere tool of capitalist growth. The financialization of capitalism has made finance the very ground of accumulation, as Christian Marazzi has explained in *The Violence of Financial Capitalism* (2010) and other recent works.

In the sphere of semiocapitalism, financial signs are not only signifiers pointing to particular referents. The distinction between sign and referent is over. The sign is the thing, the product, the process. The "real" economy and financial expectations are no longer distinct spheres. In the past, when riches were created in the sphere of industrial production, when finance was only a tool for the mobilization of capital investment in the field of material production, recovery could not be limited to the financial sphere. It also took employment and demand. Industrial capitalism could not grow if society did not grow. Nowadays, we must accept the idea that financial capitalism can recover and thrive without social recovery. Social life has become residual, redundant, irrelevant.

The financial cycle is bleeding the social environment dry: sucking energies, resources, and the future. And giving nothing back. Recovery of the financial process of valorization of capital is totally separated from the cycle of material production and social demand. Financial capitalism has achieved autonomy from social life.

Let's consider the political side of the same problem. Once upon a time, when society was suffering the blows of recession, workers reacted with strikes, struggle, and political organization, forcing state intervention to increase demand. Industrial growth needed mass consumption and social stability. What is remarkable in the ongoing crisis, on the contrary, is the widespread passivity of the workers, their inability to unionize. The political trend in Europe is the meltdown of leftist parties and the labor movement. In the US, Obama is daily attacked by racist and populist mobs, but no progressive social movement is emerging. There have been millions of foreclosures in the US since the subprime swindle, but no organized reaction has surfaced. People suffer and cry alone.

In industrial capitalism's past, the working class could fight against a target that was precisely identified: the boss, the entrepreneur who owned material things like the factory and the products of his employees' labor. Today, the boss has vanished. He is fragmented into billions of financial segments, disseminated into millions of financial agents scattered all around the world. The workers themselves are part of recombinant financial capital. They are expecting future revenues from their pension fund investments. They own stock options in the enterprise exploiting their labor. They are hooked up, like a fly in a spider web: if they move, they get strangled, but if they don't move, the spider will suck their life from them. Society may rot, fall apart, agonize. It is not going to affect the political and economic stability of capitalism. What is called economic recovery is a new round of social devastation.

So the recession is over, capitalism is recovering. Nonetheless, unemployment is rising and misery is spreading. This means that financial capitalism is autonomous from society. Capitalism doesn't need workers: it just needs cellular fractals of labor, underpaid, precarious, depersonalized. Fragments of impersonal nervous energy, recombined by the network. The crisis is going to push forward technological change and the substitution of human labor with machines. The employment rate is not going to rise in the future, and productivity will increase. A shrinking number of workers will be forced to work overtime to produce more and more.

The real bubble is the work bubble. We have been working too much; we are still working too much. The human race does not need more goods, it needs a redistribution of existing goods, an intelligent application of technology and a worldwide decrease in the life-time dedicated to labor. Social energies have to be freed from their dependence on labor and returned to the fields of social affection, education, and therapy.

We should take the concept of autonomy seriously. Under present conditions autonomy means an exodus from the domain of economic law: *Out-onomy*, abandonment of the field of economic exchange, self-organization of knowledge and production in a social life that is no longer dependent on economic culture and expectations—barter, free exchange of time and competence, food self-reliance, occupation of territories in the cities, and organization of self-defense.

The fantastic collapse that has shaken the global economy since September 2008 has opened a new phase in the history of the world. After some months of amazement and confusion, the media, political institutions, and economists have started to repeat the self-reassuring mantra: recovery is coming soon. I don't know what will happen next, but I think that the word recovery means very little in the current situation. What is sure, in my opinion, is that the workers will not recover if neoliberal ideology is not abandoned, if the myth of growth is not substituted with a new narrative. Unemployment is rising everywhere and wages are falling. And the huge debt accumulated for the rescue of the banks is weighing upon the future of society.

More than ever, economic rationality is at odds with social rationality. Economic science is not part of the solution to the crisis: it is the source of the problem. The lead article in *The Economist* of July 18, 2009, was: "What went wrong with economics?" The text is an attempt to downplay the crisis of economic knowledge and the profession of economics. For neoliberal economists, the central dogma of growth, profit, and competition cannot be questioned, because it is identified with the perfect mathematical rationality of the market. And belief in the intrinsic rationality of the market is crucial in the economic theology of neoliberalism.

But the reduction of social life to the rational exchange of economic values is an obsession that has nothing to do with science. It's a political strategy aimed at identifying humans as calculating machines, at shaping behavior and perception in such a way that money becomes the only motivation for social action. But it's not an accurate description of social dynamics, the conflicts, pathologies, and irrationality of human relationships. It's an attempt to create the anthropological form of *homo calculans* that Foucault (2008) has described in his 1979/80 seminar, *The Birth of Biopolitics*.

This attempt to see human beings as calculating devices has produced cultural devastation, and has finally shown itself to be based upon flawed assumptions. Human beings do calculate, but their calculation isn't perfectly rational, because the value of goods is not determined by objective reasons, and because decisions are influenced by what Keynes called "animal spirits." In their book of the same name, Akerlof and Shiller (2009, 1) note, "We will never really understand important economic events unless we confront the fact that their causes are largely mental in nature," echoing Keynes's assumption that the rationality of the market is not perfect in itself. Akerlof and Shiller are acknowledging the crisis of neoliberal thought, but their critique is not radical enough, and does not touch the legitimacy of the economic episteme.

Animal Spirits is also the title of a book by Matteo Pasquinelli (2008). Pasquinelli deals with bodies, numbers, and parasites, and goes much deeper in his understanding of the roots of the crisis than Akerlof and Shiller: "Cognitive capitalism emerges later in the form of a parasite: it subjects social knowledge and inhibits its emancipatory potential" (93). "Beyond the computer screen, precarious workers and freelancers experience how Free Labor and competition are increasingly devouring their everyday life" (15).

Pasquinelli goes to the core of the problem: the virtualization of social production has caused the proliferation of a parasite, destroying the prerequisites of living relationships, absorbing and neutralizing the living energies of cognitive workers. The economic recession is not only the effect of financial craziness, but also the effect of the devitalization of the social field. This is why the collapse of the economic system is also the collapse of an economic epistemology that has guided politics for the last two centuries.

Economics cannot understand the depth of the crisis, because below the crisis of financial exchange there is the crisis of symbolic exchange. I mean the psychotic boom of panic, depression, and suicide, the general decline of desire and social empathy. The question that rises from the collapse is so radical that its answer cannot be found in an economic conceptual framework.

Furthermore, one must ask if economics really is a science? If the word "science" means the creation of concepts in order to understand and describe an object, economics is not a science. Its object does not exist. The objects of economics (scarcity, wage labor, and profit) do not exist before and outside the performative action of the economic episteme. Production, consumption, and daily life become part of the economic discourse when labor is detached and opposed to human activity, when it falls under the domination of capitalist rule.

The economic object does not pre-exist conceptual activity, and economic description is in fact normative. In this sense, economics is a technique, a semiotization of the world, and also a mythology, a narration. Economics is a suggestion and a categorical imperative:

> Money makes things happen. It is the source of action in the world and perhaps the only power we invest in. Life seems to depend on it. Everything within us would like to say that it does not, that this cannot be. But the Almighty Dollar has taken command. The more it is denied the more it shows itself as Almighty. Perhaps in every other respect, in every other value, bankruptcy has been declared, giving money the power of some sacred deity, demanding to be recognized. Economics no longer persuades money to behave. Numbers cannot make the beast lie down and be quiet or sit up and do tricks. At best, economics is a neurosis of money, a symptom contrived to hold the beast in abeyance…. Thus economics shares the language of psychopathology—inflation, depression, lows and highs, slumps and peaks, investments and losses. (Sordello 1983).

From the age of the enclosures in England, the economic process has been a process that produces scarcity (scarcification). The enclosures were intended to scarcify the land, the basic means of survival, so that people who so far had been able to cultivate food for their family were forced to become proletarians, then waged industrial workers. Capitalism is based on the artificial creation of need, and economic science is essentially a technique of scarcification of time, life, and food. Under conditions of scarcity, human beings are subjected to exploitation and to the domain of profit-oriented activity. After scarcifying the land (enclosures) capitalism has scarcified time itself, forcing people who don't have property beyond their own life and body, to lend their life-time to capital. Now the capitalist obsession for growth is making both water and air scarce.

Economic science is not the science of prediction: it is the technique of producing, implementing, and exacerbating scarcity and need. This is why Marx did not speak of economy, but of political economy. The technique of economic scarcification is based on a mythology, a narration that identifies wealth as property and acquisition, and subjugates the possibility of living to the lending of time and the transformation of human activity into wage labor.

In recent decades, technological change has slowly eroded the very foundations of economic science. Shifting from the sphere of production of material objects to the semiocapitalist production of immaterial goods, the economic concepts are losing their foundation and legitimacy. The basic categories of economics are becoming totally artificial.

The theoretical justification of private property, as one can read in the writings of John Locke, is based on the need for exclusive consumption. An apple must be privatized, if you want to avoid the danger that someone else might eat your apple. But what happens when goods are immaterial, infinitely replicable without cost? Thanks to digitalization and immaterialization of the production process, the economic *nomos* of private property loses its ground, its raison d'etre, and it can be imposed only by force. Furthermore, the very foundation of wages, the relationship between time needed for production and value of the product, is vanishing. The immaterialization and cognitivization of production makes it almost impossible to quantify the average time needed to produce value. Time and value become incommensurable, and violence becomes the only law able to determine price and wage.

The neoliberal school, which has opened the way to the worldwide deregulation of social production, has fostered the mythology of rational expectations in economic exchange, and has touted the idea of a self-regulated market, primarily the labor market. But self-regulation is a lie. In order to increase exploitation, and to destroy social welfare, global capitalism has used political institutions like the International Monetary Fund and the World Trade Organization, not to mention the military enforcement of the political decisions of these institutions. Far from being self-regulated, the market is militarily regulated.

The mythology of free individuals loyally competing on the basis of perfect knowledge of the market is a lie, too. Real human beings are not perfect, rational calculating machines. And the myth of rational expectations has finally crashed after the explosion of the real estate mortgage bubble. The theory of rational expectation is crucial in neoliberal thought: the economic agents are supposed to be free to choose in a perfectly rational way the best deal in selling and buying. The fraud perpetrated by the investment agencies has destroyed the lives of millions of Americans, and has exposed the theoretical swindle.

Economic exchange cannot be described as a rational game, because irrational factors play a crucial role in social life in general. Trickery, misleading information, and psychic manipulation are not exceptions, but the professional tools of advertisers, financial agents, and economic consultants.

The idea that social relationships can be described in mathematical terms has the force of myth, but it is not science, and it has nothing to do with natural law. Notwithstanding the failure of the theory, neoliberal politics are still in control of the global machine, because the criminal class that has seized power has no intention of stepping down, and because the social brain is unable to recompose and find the way to self-organization. I read in the *New York Times* on September 6, 2009:

> After the mortgage business imploded last year, Wall Street investment banks began searching for another big idea to make money. They think they may have found one.

> The bankers plan to buy "life settlements," life insurance policies that ill and elderly people sell for cash—$400,000 for a $1 million policy, say, depending on the life expectancy of the insured person. Then they plan to "securitize" these policies, in Wall Street jargon, by packaging hundreds or thousands together

into bonds. They will then resell those bonds to investors, like big pension funds, who will receive the payouts when people with the insurance die.

The earlier the policyholder dies, the bigger the return—though if people live longer than expected, investors could get poor returns or even lose money.

Imagine that I buy an insurance policy on my life (something I would absolutely not do). My insurer, of course, will wish me a long life, so I'll pay the premiums for a long time, rather than him paying lots of money to my family if I die. But some enlightened finance guru has the brilliant idea of insuring the insurer. He buys the risk, and he invests in the hope that I die soon. You don't need the imagination of Philip K. Dick to guess how the story ends: financial agents will be motivated to kill me overnight.

The talk of recovery is based on necronomy, the economy of death. It's not new, as capitalism has always profited from wars, slaughters, and genocides. But now the equation becomes unequivocal. Death is the promise, death is the investment and the hope. Death is the best future that capitalism may secure.

The logic of speculation is different from the logic of spectacle that was dominant in late-modern times. Spectacle is the mirrorization of life, the transfer of life in the mirror of spectacular accumulation. Speculation is the subjugation of the future to its financial mirror, the substitution of present life with future money that will never come, because death will come first.

The lesson that we must learn from the first year of the global recession is sad: neoliberal folly is not going away, the financial high rollers will not stop their speculation, corporations will not stop their exploitation, and the political class, largely controlled by the corporate lobbies, is unwilling or unable to protect society from the final assault.

In 1996 J. G. Ballard (188) wrote: "the most perfect crime of all—when the victims are either willing, or aren't aware that they are victims." Democracy seems unable to stop the criminal class that has seized control of the economy, because the decisions are no longer made in the sphere of political opinion, but in the inaccessible sphere of economic automatism. The economy has been declared the basic standard around which decisions are made, and the economists have systematically identified the economy with the capitalist obsession of growth. No room for political choice is left, as corporate principles have become embedded in the technical fabric of language and imagination.

SINGULARITY INSURRECTION

Activism has generally conceived the process of subjectivation in terms of resistance. In the book he dedicated to Foucault, Gilles Deleuze speaks about subjectivity, and identifies processes of subjectivation and resistance: "Is not life this capacity to resist force?" (Deleuze 1988, 77). I think that it's time to ask: what if society can no longer resist the destructive effects of unbounded capitalism? What if society can no longer resist the devastating power of financial accumulation? The identification of the subject with resistance is dangerous in a certain sense. Deleuze himself has written that when we escape we are not simply escaping, but also looking for a new weapon.

We have to disentangle autonomy from resistance. And if we want to do that, we have to disentangle desire from energy. The prevailing focus of modern capitalism has been energy: the ability to produce, to compete, to dominate. A sort of *Energolatria*, a cult of energy, has dominated the cultural scene of the West from Faust to the Futurists. The ever growing availability of energy has been its dogma. Now we know that energy isn't boundless. In the social psyche of the West, energy is fading. I think we should reframe the concept and practice of autonomy from this point of view. The social body is unable to reaffirm its rights against the wild assertiveness of capital, because the pursuit of rights can never be dissociated from the exercise of force.

When workers were strong in the 1960s and 1970s, they did not restrict themselves to asking for their rights, to peaceful demonstrations of their will. They acted in solidarity, refusing to work, redistributing wealth, sharing things, services, and spaces. Capitalists, on their side, do not merely ask or demonstrate, they do not simply declare their wish; they enact it. They make things happen, they invest, disinvest, displace, they destroy and they build. Only force makes autonomy possible in the relation between capital and society. But what is force? What is force nowadays?

The identification of desire with energy has produced the identification of force with violence that turned out so badly for the Italian movement in the 1970s and 1980s. We have to distinguish energy and desire. Energy is falling, but desire has to be saved. Similarly, we have to distinguish force from violence. Fighting power with violence is suicidal or useless nowadays. How can we think of activists going against professional organizations of killers in the mold of Blackwater, Haliburton, secret services, mafias?

Only suicide has proved to be efficient in the struggle against power. And actually suicide has become decisive in contemporary history. The dark side of the multitude meets here the loneliness of death. Activist culture should avoid the danger of becoming a culture of resentment. Acknowledging the irreversibility of the catastrophic trends that capitalism has inscribed in the history of society does not mean renouncing it. On the contrary, we have today a new cultural task: to live the inevitable with a relaxed soul. To call forth a big wave of withdrawal, of massive dissociation, of desertion from the scene of the economy, of nonparticipation in the fake show of politics. The crucial focus of social transformation is creative singularity. The existence of singularities is not to be conceived as a personal way to salvation, they may become a contagious force.

"Yes we can," the slogan of Barack Obama's campaign, the three words that mobilized the hope and political energies of the American people in 2008, have a disturbing echo just one year after his victory. They sound much more like an exorcism than a promise. "Yes we can" may be read as a lapse in the Freudian sense, a sign coming from the collective subconscious, a diversion from the hidden intuition that, in fact, we *can't*. The mantra of Barack Obama has gathered the energies of the best part of the American people, and collected the best of the American cultural legacy.

But what about the results? So far, Obama has been unable to deal with global environmental threats, the effects of the geopolitical disaster produced by Cheney-Bush, the effects of the powerful lobbies imposing the interest of the corporations (for instance, of the private health insurers). When we think of the ecological catastrophe, of geopolitical threats, of economic collapse provoked by the financial politics of neoliberalism, it's hard to dispel the feeling that irreversible trends are already at work within the world machine. Political will seems paralyzed in the face of the economic power of the criminal class.

The age of modern social civilization seems on the brink of dissolution, and it's hard to imagine how society will be able to react. Modern civilization was based on the convergence and integration of the capitalist exploitation of labor and the political regulation of social conflict. The regulator State, the heir of Enlightenment and Socialism has been the guarantor of human rights and the negotiator of social equilibrium. When, at the end of a ferocious class struggle between labor and capital—and within the capitalist class itself—the financial class has seized power by destroying the legal regulation and transforming social composition, the entire edifice of modern civilization has begun to crumble.

Social Darwinist ideology has legitimized the violent imposition of the law of the strongest, and the very foundations of democracy have been reduced to rubble. This accelerated destruction of tolerance, culture, and human feelings has given an unprecedented impetus to the process of accumulation and has increased the velocity and extent of economic growth throughout the last two decades of the twentieth century. But it has also created the premises of a war against human society that is underway in the new century.

The war against society is waged at two different levels: at the economic level it is known as privatization and is based on the idea that every fragment and every cell of the biological, affective, linguistic spheres have to be turned into profit machines. The effect of this privatization is the impoverishment of daily life, the loss of sensibility in the fields of sex, communication, and human relationships, as well as the increasing inequality between a hyperrich minority and a dispossessed majority. At the social level, this war is waged in terms of criminalization and destabilization of territory and economic life. In large areas of the planet, which are getting bigger, production and exchange have become the ground of violent confrontation between military groups and criminal organizations. Slavery, blackmail, extortion, and murder are integral parts of the economic lexicon.

Scattered insurrections will take place in the coming years, but we should not expect much from them. They'll be unable to touch the real centers of power because of the militarization of metropolitan space, and they will not be able to gain much in terms of material wealth or political power. Just as the long wave of counterglobalization's moral protests could not destroy neoliberal power, so the insurrections will not find a solution, not unless a new consciousness and sensibility surfaces and spreads, changing everyday life and creating *Non*-Temporary Autonomous Zones rooted in the culture and consciousness of the global network.

Full employment is over. The world does not need so much labor and so much exploitation. A radical reduction of labor time is necessary. Basic income has to be affirmed as a right to life, independent of employment and disjoined from the lending of labor time. Competence, knowledge, and skills have to be separated from the economic context of exchange value and rethought in terms of free social activity.

We should not look at the current recession only from an economic point of view. We must see it essentially as an anthropological turning point that is going to change the distribution of world resources and world power. Europe is doomed to lose its economic privilege, as five hundred years of colonialism are ending. The debt that western people have accumulated is not only economic but also moral: the debt of oppression, violence, and genocide has to be paid now, and it's not going to be easy. A large part of the European population is not prepared to accept the redistribution of wealth that the recession will impose. Europe, stormed by waves of migration, is going to face a growing racist threat. Ethnic war will be difficult to avoid. In the US, the expectations raised by Obama's victory have been largely disappointed. But at the same time a wave of nonidentitarian, indigenous Renaissance is rising, especially in Latin America.

The privatization of basic needs (housing, transportation, food) and social services is based on the cultural identification of wealth and well-being with the amount of private property owned. In the anthropology of modern capitalism, well-being has been equated with acquisition, never with enjoyment. In the course of the social turmoil we will live through in the coming years, the identification of well-being with property has to be questioned. It's a political task, but above all it is a cultural task, and a psychotherapeutic one too.

When it comes to semiotic products, private property becomes irrelevant; in fact, it's more and more difficult to enforce. The campaigns against piracy are paradoxical because the real pirates are the corporations that are desperately trying to privatize the products of collective intelligence, and artificially trying to impose a tax on the community of producers. The products of collective intelligence are immanently common because knowledge can neither be fragmented nor privately owned. A new brand of communism was already springing from the technological transformations of digital networks, when the collapse of the financial markets and neoliberal ideology exposed the frailty of the foundations of hypercapitalism. Now we can predict a new wave of transformation from the current collapse of growth, increasing debt, and questioning of private consumption as well-being. Because of these three forces—commonality of knowledge, ideological crisis of private ownership, mandatory communalization of need—a new horizon is visible and a new landscape is going to surface. Communism is coming back.

The old face of communism, based on the will and voluntarism of an avant-garde, and the paranoid expectations of a new totality, was defeated at the end of the twentieth century and will not be resurrected. A totally new brand of communism is going to surface as a form of necessity, the inevitable outcome of the stormy collapse of the capitalist system. The communism of capital is a barbaric necessity. We must put freedom in this necessity, we need to make this necessity a conscious organized choice.

Communism is back, but we should give it a different name, because historical memory identifies this particular form of social organization with the political tyranny of a religion. The historical communism of the twentieth century was based on the idea of the primacy of totality over singularity. But the dialectical framework that defined the communist movement of the twentieth century has been completely abandoned and nobody will resurrect it.

The Hegelian ascendance played a major role in the formation of that kind of religious belief that was labeled "historicism." The *Aufhebung* (abolition of the Real to realize the Idea) is the paranoid background of the whole concept of communism. Within that dialectical framework, communism was viewed as an all-encompassing totality expected to abolish and supersede the all-encompassing capitalist totality. The subject (the will and action of the working class) was viewed as the instrument for the abolition of the old and the inauguration of the new.

The industrial working class, being external to the production of concepts, could only identify with the mythology of abolition and totalization, but the general intellect cannot do that. The general intellect does not need an expressive subject, such as the Leninist Party in the twentieth century. The political expression of the general intellect is at one with its activity of understanding and producing signs. We have abandoned the territory of dialectics in favor of the multilayered co-evolution of singularities. Capitalism is over, but it's not going to disappear. The creation of Non-Temporary Autonomous Zones will not give birth to any totalization. We are not going to witness a cathartic event of revolution, won't see the sudden breakdown of state power. In the coming years, we'll witness a sort of revolution without a subject. In order to subjectivate this revolution, we have to proliferate singularities. This, in my humble opinion, is our cultural and political task.

After abandoning the dialectics of abolition and totalization, we are now trying to build a theory of the dynamics of recombination and singularization, concepts clearly drawn from the works of Félix Guattari, particularly from his last book, *Chaosmosis*. By the word singularity, I mean the expression of a never before seen concatenation. The actor of this expression can be an individual or a collective, but also an event. We call it singularity if this actor recombines the multiple flows traversing its field of existence, following a principle that is not repetitive or referring to any pre-existing form of subjected subjectivity. By the world singularity, I mean an agency that does not follow any rule of conformity or repetition, and is not framed in any historical necessity or sequential understanding of history—it is an emergent, self-creative process.

Rather than a swift change in the social landscape, we should expect the slow surfacing of new trends: communities abandoning the field of the crumbling ruling economies, more and more individuals giving up their search for a job and creating their own networks of services.

The dismantling of industry is unstoppable for the simple reason that social life does not need industrial labor anymore. The myth of growth is going to be abandoned and people will look for new modes of wealth distribution. Singular communities will transform the very perception of well-being and wealth through a sense of frugality and freedom. The cultural revolution that we need in this transition leads from the perception of wealth as the private ownership of a growing number of goods that we cannot enjoy because we are too busy making the money needed for acquisition, to the perception of wealth as the enjoyment of an essential number of things that we can share with other people.

The deprivatization of services and goods will be made possible by this much needed cultural revolution. This will not happen in a planned and uniform way; it will rather be the effect of the withdrawal of singular individuals and communities, and the creation of an economy of shared use of common goods and services and the liberation of time for culture, pleasure, and affection. While this process expands at the margins of society, the criminal class will hang on to its power and enforce more and more repressive legislation, the majority of people will be increasingly aggressive and desperate. Ethnic civil war will spread all over Europe, wrecking the very fabric of civil life.

The proliferation of singularities (the withdrawal and building of Non-Temporary Autonomous Zones) will be a peaceful process, but the conformist majority will react violently, and this is already happening. The conformist majority is frightened by the fleeing of intelligent energy and simultaneously is attacking the expression of intelligent activity. The situation can be described as a fight between the mass ignorance produced by media totalitarianism and the shared intelligence of the general intellect.

We cannot predict what the outcome of this process will be. Our task is to extend and protect the field of autonomy, and to avoid as much as possible any violent contact with the field of aggressive mass ignorance. This strategy of nonconfrontational withdrawal will not always succeed. Sometimes confrontation will be made inevitable by racism and fascism. It's impossible to predict what should be done in the case of unwanted conflict. A nonviolent response is obviously the best choice, but it will not always be possible. The identification of well-being with private property is so deeply rooted that a barbarization of the human environment cannot be completely ruled out. But the task of the general intellect is exactly this: fleeing from paranoia, creating zones of human resistance, experimenting with autonomous forms of production using high-tech-low-energy methods—while avoiding confrontation with the criminal class and the conformist population.

Politics and therapy will be one and the same activity in the coming years. People will feel hopeless and depressed and panicky, because they are unable to deal with the post-growth economy, and because they will miss their dissolving modern identity. Our cultural task will be attending to those people and taking care of their insanity, showing them the way of a happy adaptation at hand. Our task will be the creation of social zones of human resistance that act like zones of therapeutic contagion. The development of autonomy must not be seen as *Aufhebung*, but as therapy. In this sense, it is not totalizing or intended to destroy and abolish the past. Like psychoanalytic therapy it should be considered an unending process.

WHEN OLD PEOPLE FALL IN LOVE

In the film *Cloud Nine* (*Wolke 9* is the original German title), Andreas Dresen stages a simple love story: Inge is married to Werner, but she meets and falls in love with Karl. She decides to leave her husband and live with her lover. One night, while she is sleeping in the arms of her beloved Karl, Inge receives a phone call: Werner has killed himself.

Well, so what? It's a love story, as I've said. I forgot to note something important: Inge and Werner and Karl are in their seventies. I think Dresen has made a beautiful movie. The love of old people is a subject that literature and cinema, with very few exceptions, have not recounted, a subject we know very little about, for the quite simple reason that old people have never existed. Until some decades ago, people over sixty were such a small minority that they were lonely and rare. Sometimes surrounded by an aura of respect and veneration, but more often rejected and pushed to the margins of society, and always alone, they were deprived of means for survival, unable to become a community. The extension of average life expectancy has been coupled so far with some reward for one's previous contributions to the growth of society: the right to retirement money. In the coming years in Europe, one-third of the population will join the ranks of old age. This is the generation that was born after the war, when the fulfillment of the modern promise of peace, democracy, and well-being was apparently at hand. Five hundred years of brutal capitalist expansion were supposedly alleviated by the political force of the organized workers. The generation born between 1945 and 1975 carried in its cultural background expectations of freedom and peace and justice, as if they were universal values. Of course, they are not, because universal values don't exist; they are the idealistic translation of cultural expectations produced by social relationships.

Over three decades of triumphant neoliberalism, the capitalist counteroffensive has destroyed the very conditions for the possibility of freedom and justice, imposing the brutal law of competition in the deregulated labor market and subjugating social life to the unbounded domination of profit. The generations now coming to the labor market, who grew up during the years of the capitalist counteroffensive, possess neither the memory of the past social civilization nor the political force to defend their existence from the predatory economy.

What about old people, now? We know very little about growing old and nothing about old people's emotions, their capacity for social organization, solidarity, and political force. We don't know because we have not experienced it. But now that experience is beginning. The age of senilization is here, and Europe is the place where it will first develop. Negative population growth has started in the territory of old Europe because the postwar generation has not proliferated with the same intensity of previous generations. This trend is spreading all over the world for many reasons—diffusion of contraceptives, the cult of individual realization, conscious refusal of maternity, high costs of reproduction in the urban environment—and, in Europe, it's already yielding its fruits, and we can speak of an advanced state of senility.

I don't want to speak of the economic effects of senilization, nor of the dilemmas of a society where more and more people reach the age of retirement while fewer and fewer people are in the age of producing. On this point, I want to say only this: the assertion that it's necessary to force seniors to postpone their retirement is purely a neoliberal trick aimed at prolonging the time of labor and trapping young people in unemployment and precarity.

What is interesting here for me is the cultural effect of social senility in the long run. The senilization of Europe parallels a process of massive migration that the policy of containment (*Schengen*) will not be able to stop. Migration is, in part, the push of poor people who are demanding a redistribution of the wealth that has been concentrated in Europe during five hundred years of colonialism. This is why we have to see the senilization of Europe as a facet of the redefinition of the planetary economic balance.

In the next decade, Europe will be forced to make a choice between two possibilities. One is a redistribution of wealth and resources that implies opening European borders to the crowds coming from Africa and Asia, a downsizing of western consumption, and the adoption of lifestyles heading toward the "UnGrowth" of production and consumption. The other is the intensification of an inter-ethnic civil war whose first signs are already visible in the European territory. The success of the xenophobic parties in the elections of June 2009 is one of those signs. Most Europeans are desperately defending the privilege accumulated over centuries of colonialism, but this privilege has been deteriorating since the fall of colonial empires in the past century, and is now really falling apart in the global recession. The June 2009 elections display a European sadness, the inability to deal with senility or the psycho-energetic decay of the social organism. The result at the polls is not the effect of political will, but rather the symptom of a rapidly expanding senile dementia.

During the age of modernity, a very delicate balance was created between the infosphere and reason. The political will could act rationally because this balance gave historical actors the possibility of comprehending a relatively narrow range of information and therefore of making decisions based on it. But the acceleration of semiotic emissions and the thickening of the infosphere has produced, in the long run, an effect of overload and, therefore, of anxiety and panic. At the same time, Europe has grown so old. It's a demographic problem, first of all, but it's not only demographic. Europe is a country of old people groping desperately at their lives, not out of love, but for property. A country of old people needing young nurses from the Philippines, Moldavia, and Morocco; old idiots tormented by despising the agility of those young people, people who have suffered so much at our hands that they don't fear any more suffering, and don't care about the punishment of European law. Senile dementia (loss of memory, irrational fear of the unknown) is spreading in every generational stratum of European society, mentally frail and socially tired. Young voters who vote for rightist nationalist parties are no less obtuse than the frightened elderly, just as unable to think or find a way out their conformism.

How will it end? It's easy to predict. Old Europeans are well armed and they will kill. Pogrom, mass violence, inter-ethnic civil war. This the future of Europe. We should find a way to translate in nonreligious terms the Christian concept of "resignation." What is to be done when nothing can be done, when too much hate has accumulated in the collective karma? How can we continue being happy and free when we understand that a war machine is hidden in every niche? This is the question that I am addressing to myself, to my friends, and to my generation—the generation born after the last war fought by young people, before senility took hold of us, making a pacific wisdom possible, or pushing us toward the abyss of aggressive dementia.

The generation that grew up in the decades of postwar hope is today facing a huge cultural task, no less important than the task we were able to carry out in 1968. Now we need to create the conditions for European society to consciously start a process of UnGrowth, and to repay the immense debt that western society has accumulated during five hundred years of colonialism.

The current recession is a consequence of the financial debt that the West (especially the US) has taken on during recent decades. But there's also a much heavier debt that cannot in any way be repaid. It is the symbolic debt that comes from the genocide of the native populations of America, and from the deportation and enslavement of millions of human beings from Africa and Asia.

The senile generation of Europe may become the subject of a cultural revolution to prepare western society for a long-lasting agreement on the redistribution of wealth and resources. Such a cultural revolution should start with a critique of the energetic juvenilism permeating modern culture. The ideology of unbounded growth and the cult of aggressive competition are the foundations of capitalist development; they also nourished the romantic and nationalist ideologies that have aggressively mobilized western society in late-modern times.

A senile culture aspiring to UnGrowth and the reduction of the consumerist push, on the activation of solidarity and sharing, seems today—I must concede—a very unlikely possibility. The elections have shown that the European population is determined to defend its privilege with all the means at hand. But this stance cannot bring anything good, and is already bringing a lot of evil. An inter-ethnic civil war is hiding in daily life, and we are going to see it explode with unimaginable violence. Young people accustomed to very difficult living conditions are surrounding the fortress. They are bearing the unconscious memory of centuries of exploitation and humiliation; they are also bearing the conscious expectation of those things that advertising and global ideology have promised to them.

During past decades, Europe was looking like the continent of peace and social justice. Now it's sinking in a wave of sadness and cynicism. Young people seem unable to change social conditions, and are wandering in a labyrinth of a society without solidarity or relaxation. The senile population could be the bearer of a new hope, if they are able to face the inevitable with a relaxed soul. They could discover something that humankind has never known: the love of the aged, the sensuous slowness of those who do not expect anything better from life than wisdom, the wisdom of those who have seen much, forgotten nothing, but look at everything as if for the first time.

HAPPY END

I'm often invited to lecture about the subjects I deal with in this book. The audience is generally composed of social activists, radical thinkers, and artists. Although the discussions that follow my talks are generally lively and the participation intense, by the end I sometimes feel a sense of bitterness in my audience. I share this sense of malaise, and easily guess the reason for it: my argument does not have a happy ending.

It's true, I don't have a happy ending for my fabulation. I don't see any discernable subjectivation, resurrection of consciousness, or emancipatory forms in the foreseeable future. And I don't like to cheat at this game. I don't like empty words of self-reassurance, or rhetoric about the multitude. I prefer to tell the truth, at least, the limited truth as I see it: there is no way out, social civilization is over, the neoliberal precarization of labor and the media dictatorship have destroyed the cultural antibodies that, in the past, made resistance possible. As far as I know.

But I only know what I can see from my limited point of observation, of course. During the twentieth century, the moral revolt against exploitation was based on the reasonable prospect of society's autonomy from the cultural and economic domination of capitalist rule. This prospect was based on a realistic approach to the analysis of existing conditions.

Then something changed. During the past few decades, I've witnessed the mutation induced by the capitalist economy, and I've decided that this mutation is irreversible: it hasn't only affected the social sphere, but also the semiotic, biological, and psychic spheres.

Therefore, my knowledge and my understanding disown the possibility of an alternative, of an escape from the hell emerging as the legacy of thirty years of unfettered capitalist rule.

The dissociation of capitalism and modernity is complete: capitalist rule is getting rid of modern civilization. Humanism, Enlightenment, Socialism, the cultural regulators of modern democracy, have been swept away by the cultural deregulation implied in the capitalist final assault. Privatization of every living space and activity, competition and economic brutality in the social sphere, have deeply affected the self-perception of the social body. In my knowledge and my understanding, this process now seems inevitable and irreversible, because it has not only destroyed the structures of social civilization that modernity created, but it has also jeopardized the affective fabric of the social environment and the cultural expectations of the new generation.

This is what I see, what I think, and this is what I say, so I understand the dissatisfaction of the activists who gather to attend my lectures. They seem to ask: "So, why resist? What is the point of radical thought, what's the point of critique and intellectual engagement, if you think that no conscious collective subjectivation is possible, and no way to hijack the criminal train of capitalism?"

In these final pages, I want to answer this question.

In 1992, Félix Guattari published his last book, *Chaosmosis*. It is about schizoanalysis, and also about how the political and environmental landscape was getting more and more catastrophic in those final years of the century. Here is the problem Guattari sets himself:

> Among the fogs and miasmas which obscure our *fin de millénaire,* the question of subjectivity is now returning as a leitmotiv. It is not a natural given any more than air or water. How do we produce it, capture it, enrich it, and permanently reinvent it in a way that renders it compatible with Universes of mutant value? How do we work for its liberation, that is, for its resingularization? (Guattari 1995, 135).

Guattari is wondering here about the possibility of a process of liberation, defining liberation as "resingularization." He also speaks of fogs and miasmas. After the illusion of peace that followed the crash of the Soviet empire, a chaotic war exploded in the Persian Gulf. The Cold War geopolitical order was over and the new conflict was a symptom of a general chaos in world relations.

In 1992, in order to make some decisions about the global environment, a summit of the leading nations of the world was called in Rio de Janeiro. On that occasion George Bush senior informed the world that the American lifestyle was non-negotiable, and the Americans refused to talk about the environmental catastrophe. The Rio de Janeiro summit was a failure, and it opened the way to the present environmental chaos.

When Félix Guattari died, some months after the Rio de Janeiro summit, he was conscious of the extreme dangers of the world situation. In the last years of his life, he experienced the double black hole of internal and external chaos. In the black hole that psychiatrists call depression, we can never distinguish among the personal, the social, and the planetary. Peoples, races, mobs are always there in the mental landscape of schizo-consciousness (and unconsciousness).

This is my starting point about chaos: the world-chaos that Guattari talks about in his last book is not only depression, fog, and miasma. Chaos is much more than this. It's also the infinity of colors, dazzling lights, hyperspeed intuitions, and breathtaking emotions.

Chaos is a twofold word: in the last book they wrote together (*What Is Philosophy?*), Guattari and Deleuze say that Chaos is both friend and foe. It's both enemy and ally: "It is as if the *struggle against chaos* does not take place without an affinity with the enemy" (Deleuze and Guattari 1994, 203).

Chaos is an enemy, but it can also become a friend, because chaos is the door of creation. We are walking in darkness, but we are able to create concepts that illuminate the surroundings.

Friendship is one of the keywords of this last book by Deleuze and Guattari. Friendship means sharing a refrain, a semiotic set that allows us to see the same vision and helps to create a world out of chaos.

Chaos is not in the world; reality knows neither chaos nor order. Chaos is in the relationship between the speed of our brain and the changing speed of reality. Chaos is a complexity that is too dense, too thick, too intense, too speedy, too fast, too much for our brains to decipher. We speak of chaos when our speed of psychic elaboration is overwhelmed by the speed and the complexity of the world.

Chaos chaotizes, disentangles any consistency into infinite pieces. But the task of philosophy is the creation of planes of consistency without losing the infinity out of which thought arises.

The chaos we are dealing with has both a mental and a physical existence—not the physical existence of the world, but the physical existence of the organism (as a conscious and sensitive entity). The physical existence of the body is the space where chaos arises and takes place. In this space of unhappiness and mental disorder, of panic, depression, and loneliness, the projected order of the world collapses.

Chaos is too complex an environment to be decoded by the available explanatory grids, it is an environment in which semiotic and emotional flows are circulating too fast for our minds to elaborate.

The elaboration of chaos is made possible by the emergence of a semiogenetic machine that Guattari calls a *refrain*. This is chaosmosis, the emergence of a form: creative morphogenesis.

The morphogenetic process has long been described in deterministic terms by modern epistemology: Newton and Galileo founded physics on the idea that a unifying language—the language of Mathematics—frames the whole of creation. The final goal of theoretical and scientific work was the understanding of laws that describe the determinist generation of any natural process. Biology and biogenetics have developed in the same deterministic frame: they describe biological morphogenesis in terms of a deterministic relation between the code and the organism. Following the discovery of DNA in the 1950s, the body has been conceived of as development and realization of the code, an implied order that accounts for the unfolding of life.

This vision of nature went along with the social episteme of the nineteenth and twentieth centuries, which was based on a deterministic relationship between economic factors and social effects. The epistemological framework based on determinism has been fertile in the modern age, in the sense that the mechanical paradigm has been useful to understand a world that was based on industrial production and mechanical technologies. But the acceleration that electronic technologies have imposed on production and knowledge has opened a new dimension that cannot be described in deterministic terms. Determinism fails to understand the fuzzy, hypercomplex organization of the network of cognitive labor: the relation between labor time and value is dissolved, and the very idea of determination fades.

The uncertainty principle, first asserted by Heisenberg in the field of microphysics, frames the new social consciousness.

Just as in microphysics you cannot determine the moment and the speed of a particle, because the presence of the observer alters the picture, so too in sociology you cannot determine the relation between the present and the future, because the subjective factor is too complex to be understood and described.

At the present moment, the predictive power of knowledge is at stake. The global mind's complexity is beyond the understanding of the situated mind of any individual, group, party, or state.

Marxism has long been understood as a form of predictive science. Being able to analyze the relationship between different social actors (bourgeoisie and working class), being able to predict the dynamics of economic crises (overproduction, fall of the profit rate, breakdown of the capitalist economy), the scholastic vision of Marxism claimed to also predict the outcome of the story: the final victory of communism, the abolition of classes, and the realization of reason. In the official version of dialectical materialism (Diamat), inherited from Hegel and reformulated by Engels, the relationship between the present condition and the future was explained in terms of a deterministic reduction. The future was imagined as the unfurling of a tendency inscribed in the present. Repetition prevailed, and difference was ignored. The faith in a progressive future was based on this deterministic reduction, and it evaporated as soon as that conceptual framework was abandoned.

The event is not predictable because it is not the development of what we presently know. The event is a creative gesture creating a new *refrain*.

So, I answer the question: why resist, why persist in seeking autonomy from power? Where is the hope? The hope is in the limits of my knowledge and understanding. My knowledge and understanding don't see how any development of the social catastrophe could cultivate social well-being. But the catastrophe (in the etymology of *kata* and *strophein*) is exactly the point where a new landscape is going to be revealed.

I don't see that landscape because my knowledge and my understanding are limited, and the limits of my language are the limits of my world. My knowledge and understanding miss the event, the singularity. So I must act "as if." As if the forces of labor and knowledge might overcome the forces of greed and of proprietary obsession. As if the cognitive workers might overcome the fractalization of their life and intelligence, and give birth to the self-organization of collective knowledge. I must resist simply because I cannot know what will happen after the future, and I must preserve the consciousness and sensibility of social solidarity, of human empathy, of gratuitous activity—of freedom, equality, and fraternity. Just in case, right? Just because we don't know what is going to happen next, in the empty space that comes after the future of modernity. I must resist because this is the only way to be in peace with myself. In the name of self-love, we must resist. And self-love is the basic ethical rule that an anarchist prizes.

The present ignorance has to be seen as the space of a possibility. We have to start from the ignorance of the general intellect. The force of collective intelligence is boundless. Theoretically. But it currently lacks any consciousness of itself. Intelligence without self-consciousness.

I am talking about the self-consciousness of the general intellect, millions and millions of people worldwide producing the infoflow that makes the planet go around. Creating a form of self-consciousness of the general intellect is the political task of the future. And it is not only political, but philosophical, epistemological, and, in the end, therapeutic.

Poetry and therapy (thera-poetry) will be the forces leading to the creation of a cognitarian self-consciousness: not a political party, not the organization of interests, but the reactivation of the cognitarian sensibility.

The ignorance of the general intellect is the starting point, after the future.

Why are the cognitariat weak and disunited and unable to assert their rights as laborers, their knowledge as researchers? Because they live in a bifurcated form, because their brain is detached from their body, because their communication communicates less and less, while more and more freezing sensitivity to life. The new space of activism is here, in the connection of poetry, therapy, and the creation of new paradigms.

AFTER FUTURISM

One hundred years ago Filippo Tommaso Marinetti published the manifesto that introduced the century that believed in the future. The 1909 *Futurist Manifesto*, which you can find in the first pages of this book, expounds the becoming-machine of mankind. This becoming-machine reached its finale with the concatenations of the global Web. It has now been overturned by the crisis of a financial system that was founded on the futurization of the economy, debt, and economic promise. The promise is over. The era of post-future has begun.

MANIFESTO OF POST-FUTURISM
Franco Berardi

1. We sing of the danger of love, the daily creation of a sweet energy that is never dispersed.

2. The essential elements of our poetry will be irony, tenderness, and rebellion.

3. Ideology and advertising have exalted the permanent mobilization of the productive and nervous energies of humankind toward profit and war. We exalt tenderness, sleep, and ecstasy, the frugality of needs and the pleasure of the senses.

4. We declare that the splendor of the world has been enriched by a new beauty: the beauty of autonomy. Each to her own rhythm; nobody should be constrained to march at a uniform pace. Cars have lost their allure of rarity and, above all, they can no longer perform the task for which they were conceived. Speed has slowed down. Cars are as immobile as stupid slumbering tortoises in the city traffic. Only slowness is fast.

5. We sing of the men and the women who caress one another to know one another and the world better.

6. The poet must expend herself with warmth and prodigality to increase the power of collective intelligence and reduce the time of wage labor.

7. Beauty exists only in autonomy. No work that fails to express the intelligence of the possible can be a masterpiece. Poetry is a bridge cast over the abyss of nothingness to allow the sharing of different imaginations and to free singularities.

8. We are on the extreme promontory of the centuries. We must look behind us to remember the abyss of violence and horror that military aggressiveness and nationalist ignorance is capable of conjuring up at any moment. We have lived in the stagnant time of religion for too long. Omnipresent and eternal speed is already behind us, in the Internet, so we can forget its syncopated rhymes and find our singular rhythm.

9. We ridicule the idiots who spread the discourse of war: the fanatics of competition, the fanatics of the bearded gods who incite massacres, the fanatics terrorized by the disarming femininity blossoming in all of us.

10. We demand that art turn into a life-changing force. We seek to abolish the separation between poetry and mass communication, to reclaim the power of media from the merchants and return it to the poets and the sages.

11. We sing of the great crowds who can finally free themselves from the slavery of wage labor through collective revolt against exploitation. We sing of the infinite web of knowledge and invention, the immaterial technology that frees us from physical hardship. We sing of the rebellious cognitariat who are in touch with their bodies. We sing to the infinity of the present and abandon the illusion of a future.

AN
INTERVIEW
WITH
BIFO

franco "bifo" berardi, gary genosko, and nicholas thoburn

SPRING 2010

NICK: Your politics and writing in associations like *A/traverso*, Radio Alice, Telestreet, and Rekombinant has been entwined with media practice. I'm very interested in the way that your work here has tended to break with the dominant political media model of "counterinformation"—one *A/Traverso* text, for instance, talks of Radio Alice enacting a "break in the relationship between broadcasting and the making known of facts." Instead, you have politicized media form itself, attending to the associational, affective, asignifying, sensory properties of media. In *After the Future*, you write about the Russian Futurist "transrational" language of *zaum*, which communicates affects and intensities rather than meanings as such, and Radio Alice is said to have opened radio to the "unstated" and the "uncanny," making language "tactile" and "unproductive." Can you tell us when and why you first started paying attention to media form as a site of political practice?

BIFO: During the 1970s, in Italy social conflicts broke the established forms of political organization. At the same time, autonomous movements of young workers and students started speaking a language that was different from the legacy of twentieth century ideological language. In May 1975, with a small group of friends—students, militants, feminists, workers, and poets—I launched a magazine called *A/traverso*.

We wanted to create a new form of political communication. We had been reading Burroughs and Deleuze and Guattari, we had been listening to a lot of rock music, and our magazine was intended to bring into social communication the spirit of the artistic avant-garde, Dadaism and Futurism, Surrealism, and beat generation poetry.

In 1976, the free radio movement broke out, Radio Alice started ed broadcasting in February of that year. If you want to understand the effect that free radio produced in the mediascape of those years, consider that the infosphere was quite empty at that time. Only the state-owned RAI was allowed to air its messages. The voices of the Demo-Christian State and the Vatican dominated the airwaves and the imagination of the people. So, it was hence easy for us to find an audience. Those who had never had a voice in the mediascape could finally have their say.

Free radio helped a lot in the creation of a new culture: the autonomous culture of the young workers who expressed their refusal of industrial work. Their sensibility was free from the legacy of the modern work ethic. This was the expression of the legacy of the avant-garde of the twentieth century, but at the same time it was the announcement of a postindustrial society and the new cognitive labor.

The history of struggle in the field of the infosphere and the mediascape is an exciting history in Italy. The liberalization of broadcasting—initiated by a verdict of the Constitutional Court stating the unconstitutionality of the state-owned monopoly—led to a proliferation of free radio stations. But the next step was the creation of a financial empire based on television and advertising. Berlusconi, owner of Publitalia, an advertising company based in Milan, launched the TV channel Canale 5 in the late 1970s. It was the beginning of the Berlusconi empire, which has changed Italian culture and politics so deeply. In the 1980s, commercial television took the place of free radio in the production of the social imagination. The entire process of deregulation is encompassed in this passage. From liberalization to privatization; from the engagement of social energies in the field of communication to the privatization of the media.

NICK: You've worked in print media, radio, television, mailing lists, and other digital mediums. What capacities and constraints have these different mediums presented for a politics of media form?

BIFO: Working as an activist in the fields of radio and the Internet have much in common. Free radio stations started using the telephone in their broadcasting. It was new. For the first time, the audience could intervene. The interactive spirit of the Net was already alive in the experience of free radio.

Television is a totally different place, a different relationship to the audience. TV is essentially centric, although it tries to incorporate interactive techniques. Television immobilizes people and saturates their attention up to a point of mental subjugation.

I've had two experiences with TV broadcasting. The first, between 1995 and 2000, was a program broadcast by RAI 3 (the cultural channel of the national public television station). The name of the program was *Mediamente*. It was about the emerging Netculture and digital technologies, new lifestyles and new social values. It was an interesting experience, but it was brutally ended in 2001, when Berlusconi won the political elections. The political blackmail was intolerable; they wanted me to do things I didn't like. I gave up and resigned.

Then I took part in an experiment called Telestreet. In 2002, trying to counter the Berlusconi dictatorship in the field of TV broadcasting, we called upon activists nationwide to create their own TV stations on a very, very local scale: a street, a neighborhood, a building, a school. Telestreet proliferated all over Italy between 2002 and 2003.

At the end of 2002, almost two hundred small TV stations took part in a Telestreet meeting in Bologna. However, this project couldn't survive for long, because producing TV is impossible in the long run, if you don't have money. The energy of Telestreet in its first period was generated by many video-activists who wanted to show their productions. But by 2005, the flow of video-activism had taken the path of YouTube; we could say that Web 2.0 killed the Telestreet experiment.

You see the difference between radio and TV. A radio station can survive with small amounts of money. On the contrary, TV cannot be turned into a democratic medium. It's undemocratic in its very paradigm and conception.

NICK: I want to raise for discussion the theme of "communism." Leaving your specific practice in Potere Operaio aside for a moment, can you tell us how you first came to communist politics, and if there are any currents in Marxism that have been especially influential on your political and intellectual development?

BIFO: I joined the FGCI (youth organization of the Italian Communist Party) in 1964, when I was only fourteen years old. My father, who had fought in the Second World War as a partisan against the Nazis, was a Communist and a teacher, and had exposed me to Marxist philosophy since my childhood. He also suggested that I read Schopenhauer, Kierkegaard, and many other authors, but Marx was the most influential, as you can guess.

As a young militant of the Communist Party I became a high school student organizer. Then, in 1967, I was expelled from the Party, because I was accused of being too close to Maoism. I've never, in fact, been a Maoist but this was the obsession of the prosoviet Communists in the 1960s, so they decided I was a Maoist and sent me off.

In that period, actually, I was consorting with the intellectual group of Potere Operaio. As far as my Marxist formation is concerned, I started studying the regular books of the communist militant, especially Marx's economic and philosophical writings of 1844. But when I discovered the heterodox magazines *Quaderni Rossi* and *Classe Operaia*, and the seminal book by Tronti, *Operai e capitale*, I started thinking that the real problem was not the political organization of the Party, but cultural change, change in the social composition of labor. I can say that the most influential texts of my formative years were "The Fragment on Machines" from the *Grundrisse*, which was published in *Quaderni Rossi*, and a text by Romano Alquati concerning labor force and class composition in the experience of the northern Italian factory, Olivetti ("*Forza lavoro and composizione di classe all'Olivetti di Ivrea*"), also published in *Quaderni Rossi*.

NICK: I would be intrigued to hear if you have had any relation to the Italian Communist Left associated with Amadeo Bordiga? It strikes me that Bordiga's remarkable work in the 1950s on the capitalist structure of technology, his reading of Marx's *Grundrisse*, his critique of democracy and "self-management," and so on, displays striking points of resonance with operaismo (not that there aren't also clear and important points of divergence). Yet there appears to have been little or no exchange between these currents.

BIFO: Bordiga is a very interesting case of denial in the history of the Italian workers' movement. He has been erased from the history of the Party and from the history of Italian culture. Not only was he the first General Secretary of the Italian Communist Party, expelled in the name of Stalinist orthodoxy, but he was also an original thinker, and has some interesting consonance with the ideas that Potere Operaio supported in the 1960s. The most interesting thing in Bordiga's outlook is his radical refusal of any identification between the interests of the working class and the national interest. Bordiga's assertion of a radical irreducibility of workers' interests, the refusal of any general interest of the nation, of the people, of the country, is very much in the vein of the Trontian "rude razza pagana" (rude, pagan race), as he labels the industrial working class.

NICK: You mention *Quaderni Rossi* and *Classe Operaia*; did you have any involvement with these early incarnations of operaismo, with people like Raniero Panzieri?

BIFO: I was part of a younger generation, and never met Panzieri. I was eighteen years old in 1968, when the whole experience of *Quaderni Rossi* and *Classe Operaia* was over. I met Negri in Potere Operaio and worked with him and many others after 1967.

NICK: Turning to your experiences in Potere Operaio, it's clear that this was a hugely inventive and intense conjunction of people, ideas, and politics that had a great impact on the unfurling of workers' politics over the course of the 1970s and, indeed, beyond. A good deal has been written about the political orientations and concepts of this group, but can you share your impressions of the atmosphere, culture, or style of Potere Operaio as an organization?

BIFO: My feeling was not of taking part in a political action, strategy, direction, or organization. I had much more the feeling of playing the role of the fortune teller, of the cartographer who reads signs of the future in the words of young workers coming out from the factory, who tries to sketch out possibilities and connections, and spells words and concepts in order to make the process understandable. Potere Operaio for me was much more a group of social artists than a group of politicians.

NICK: Then there is the crucial development in May 1973 when Potere Operaio abolishes itself as an organization so as to become immersed in the base structures of the emerging movement of autonomia. To me, this displays a crucial feature of non-Leninist communism, which interprets the existence of a distinct and enduring organizational faction more as a sign of movement weakness than strength. Nonetheless, the internal and external pressures of the vanguard-form—what Guattari analyses through the concept of the "subjected group"—are such that the group tends to develop its own momentum and rigidity, making dissolution a difficult task. You yourself have noted in the essay "Anatomy of Autonomy" that, as the new radicalism of autonomia developed, the revolutionary groups displayed an "inexorable bureaucratization." Can I ask you, then, how did the decision to dissolve Potere Operaio come about? How did you experience the group's end?

BIFO: When Potere Operaio decided to dissolve I was already out. I had left the organization in 1971, two years before the official dissolution. In that year, the leaders of the group turned Leninist, and they decided to act as a militant party; I disagreed with them. I published my first book, *Contro il lavoro*, in order to distance myself from the Leninist evolution, then I left. Therefore, you can imagine that I agreed with the decision to dissolve the group in 1973. I thought that social autonomy in the factories and in social life did not need any external direction.

NICK: All of this was a time—the late 1960s, the 1970s—when communism was very much in the air. What does it mean to you to be a communist *today*, when this figure has considerably less purchase on the popular imagination?

BIFO: Communism is a difficult word to use. It reminds us of the experiment in the foundation of a new totality, the dialectical negation, the inauguration of a totally new world. This experiment has been a failure. Lenin's conception, and the triumph of the Communist State in Russia, stiffened social dynamics throughout the century, and weakened rather than strengthened the social autonomy of workers in the world. I prefer to think in terms of autonomy and lines of escape from the established domination of capital.

NICK: Yet communism is not dead and buried. It is remarkable that a recent London conference, "On The Idea of Communism," drew a crowd of 900 plus, and it was by no means a passive audience, expressing some frustration at the parameters of communism there displayed. Many people, I would suggest, are eager to engage with what communist politics might be today.

BIFO: I did not attend the conference, so I cannot talk about it. But I'm not sure that a large audience at the conference is proof that communism is alive. Anyway, I think that drawing any continuity with the historical legacy of the twentieth century today is of no use. There is no conceptual or political reason to stress the relation with the communist past.

The final neoliberal offensive, the financial dictatorship, the systematic destruction of the infrastructures of social civilization are growing concerns, and there is rage in a large part of the population. But this rage is impotent and inconsequential, as consciousness and coordinated action seem beyond the reach of present society. Look at the European crisis. Never in our life have we faced a situation so charged with revolutionary opportunities. Never in our life have we been so impotent. Never have intellectuals and militants been so silent, so unable to find a way to show a new possible direction.

Why? Because the historical process has totally exceeded human will and human understanding. Humans are overwhelmed, unable to control the hyperspeed and hypercomplex infosociety that has absorbed the historical dimension. The creation of a collective consciousness seems to be far beyond the reach of the metropolitan precarious cognitariat, who are unable to create the cultural conditions for solidarity.

I very much agree with Mark Fisher in *Capitalist Realism*: "British students seem resigned to their fate. But this is a matter not of apathy, nor of cynicism, but of reflexive impotence. They know things are bad, but more than that, they know they can't do anything about it. But that 'knowledge', that reflexivity, is not a passive observation of an already existing state of affairs. It is a self-fulfilling prophecy."

The origin of this impotence lies in the growing disparity between the speed of infoflow and the slowness of human reactivity (which implies culture, affectivity, corporeality, disease). Nature explodes. The volcano erupting in Iceland is a metaphor of the sudden return of the unconscious (corporeality of the planet, corporeality of affects), it disrupts the flow of transportation and the interconnection of the European brain becomes hectic, frantic, and finally inefficient. International meetings are interrupted. International fairs go empty. Tourism cracks. Technology fails to contain the energy of overexploited Nature. The hubris of the most powerful corporations, BP and Halliburton, and the nemesis of the gigantic oil spill in the Mexican Gulf.

In the Euro-chaos, Nature seems not to play any role. Only figures, zeroes and ones. But the problem is the same. Human will has become unable to process the exploding complexity of its own products, to understand, predict, and manage the info-overflow, and the intricacies of the ever-changing network, the virtual infrastructure of the swarm, the soul of the swarm.

It's not the good will or the bad will of human actors, but the automatic interoperation of abstract functions that holds together and suddenly breaks the continuum of social life. Monetary dogma has incorporated into social relations an abstract model of interdependencies and compatibilities that makes the system operational. Any break in the flow produces effects of self-protection in the system. Positive feedback. When a system exposed to a perturbation acts in such a way to increase the magnitude of the perturbation, we speak of "positive feedback." This is what happens in the sphere of neoliberal economy: the more neoliberal politics destroys life, environment, wealth, and welfare, the more the ruling class strengthens neoliberal rule.

What can be done in such a situation? What political methodology should we follow? Demonstrations and protests are no use. Democratic elections are no use, as the leaders elected by people have to respond to monetary authority and the financial algorithm.

Only withdrawal, passivity, abandonment of the labor market, of the illusions of full employment and a fair relation between labor and capital, can open a new way. Only self-reliant communities leaving the field of social competition can open a way to a new hope. This is why I prefer to say "autonomy" rather than "communism." Autonomy does not refer to creating a new totality, nor to a general subversion of the present, but to the possibility of escape, of self-reliance. Autonomy means reduction of contacts with the economic sphere.

NICK: I have a great deal of sympathy with your critique of activism and militancy. The recent return to the figure of the militant—in circles influenced by Badiou and Žižek for example—is certainly challenging and provocative in the face of neoliberal consensus and the cynicism of democratic politics. Nonetheless, it seems that this move has missed or deliberately ignored the radical critique of the repressive structure of militant subjectivity that characterized the leading edge of post-'68 political culture (including Deleuze and Guattari, but also left communism, antipsychiatry, and socialist feminism). Moreover, the new conditions of the production of subjectivity—associated with the expanded media sphere, digital communications networks, disaggregated and precarious labor, the rise of psychopharmacology, mass modulation of affect, and so on—leave a politics founded on militant consciousness and will somewhat lacking in purchase on the real conditions of life.

In contrast, your work here crucially asks that we face up to the radically changed social situation, and with sober senses—in an interview with Giuseppina Mecchia you state that today a leftist "optimism of the will seems to me a kind of hysterical reflex." But isn't there a danger that "withdrawal," "passivity," and "self-reliant communities"—the terms you use above—lead to a self-enclosed subjectivity, an isolation against the outside world, with the conservatism and moralism that this can entail?

BIFO: I think that the long-lasting neoliberal rule has eroded the cultural and material bases of social civilization, which was the progressive core of modernity. And this is irreversible. We have to face it. The mutation produced by global capital intermingled with recombinant technologies cannot be undone. In this context, passivity does not mean ethical resignation, but refusal of participation. Capitalism is demanding participation, collaboration, active intervention in the economy, competition and entrepreneurship, critical consumption, constructive critique. All this is fake. Activism is fake, when no horizon can be seen. Radical passivity means active withdrawal, and withdrawal means creation of spaces of autonomy where solidarity can be rebuilt, and where self-relying communities can start a process of proliferation, contagion, and eventually, of reversal of the trend. I don't see any conservatism or moralism in this, just the acknowledgment of the dead end we are facing after thirty years of economic subjugation and profit worshipping.

NICK: Staying with your critique of activism, in *After the Future* you make moves toward a political practice of "exhaustion." It reminds me of a comment Deleuze makes about Guattari, that amidst the whirlwind of Guattari's life he also had a "passion for returning to zero." You've written some very interesting and moving lines about the place of depression in Guattari's life and work. Have you also found resources in Guattari for thinking about a nonactivist approach to politics, a politics of exhaustion?

BIFO: Actually the problem of depression and of exhaustion is never elaborated in an explicit way by Guattari. I see here a crucial problem of the theory of desire: the denial of the problem of limits in the organic sphere. I mean, the problem is that the organism is intrinsically limited, and when you speak of subjectivation you are not only speaking of enunciation, but also of the organic dimension of the enunciator.

The notion of the "body without organs" hints at the idea that the organism isn't something that you can define, that the organism is a process of exceeding, of going beyond a threshold, of "becoming other." This is a crucial point, but it's also a dangerous point.

Subjectivation means "becoming other," and this process has no limit, you can always shift and go elsewhere, and become other, and other, and other. It's okay, but you also have to answer the question: who is becoming other? The subject does not pre-exist the process of becoming, that's true. But the physical and nervous matter of the body, this cannot be separated from the process of becoming itself.

What body, what mind is going through transformation and becoming? Which invariant lies under the process of becoming other? If you want to answer this question you have to acknowledge death, finitude, and depression. Here is the problem of the limit, the problem of irreversibility, the problem of death.

GARY: Guattari comments on his use of Gamma-OH in the early 1970s as an antidepressant and socialibilizer. It was not especially effective, but did show that he was taking some measures to deal with depression during the *Anti-Oedipus* years. However, Guattari's drug use was closely linked to issues in amorous relations at a number of different points in his life. What do you know about this drug and Guattari's use of it?

BIFO: I don't know about this drug, but I remember that in the last years of his life, sometimes Guattari told me: I'm taking drugs in order to become stupid. He was joking with his own depression, with his experience of the black hole.

The way Guattari considered drugs was very interesting. I remember the first time I walked with him in La Borde clinic. He gave pills to some of the people who were recovering there, and I asked him why do you do that? Don't you think that chemical drugs are bad?

And he answered, what do you have against chemistry? Actually, he refused the idea that there is a radical discontinuity between chemistry and Nature, a radical discontinuity between the mechanosphere and the noosphere, sociosphere, and infosphere. It's all part of the same process of heterogeneous becoming.

GARY: In the mid 1980s, you were involved in a group called Topia, which Guattari praised for its work in the promotion of singularity and the development of antitechnocratic mental ecologies. Now, Guattari did this in the context of alt-psychiatric movements. Can you explain what this little-known group Topia was interested in? Did you get involved with alt-psychiatry in Italy? Were you conversant with Franco Basaglia and other institutional experimenters in Italy in the alternative treatment stream—whether this was in the mental hospital, prison, or factory or school?

BIFO: Topia was the name of a large space which once upon a time had been a textile factory. In 1985, I rented this place with some friends who were psychologists, and electronic programmers and artists.

The idea was to create a center for the ecology of mind, a space for schizotherapy and theater, visual arts and infotechnology. In that period, I was strongly influenced by Gregory Bateson, and the relationship between art therapy and new technology was the core of our experiment. Guattari came there and gave a lecture.

As far as concerns my relation with the Italian antipsychiatric movement, during my university years I studied with Gianfranco Minguzzi, a Bolognese psychologist who was one of the main theoreticians of the antipsychiatric movement, so I was aware of the importance of Franco Basaglia's work, at the theoretical and political level, but I never personally met him.

The 1977 movement in Bologna was conscious of the political importance of a nonauthoritarian approach to psychopathology, and many of the students of the movement in the 1970s had been reading *Psychoanalyse et transversalité*, the first of Guattari's books published in Italy, which was dedicated to the relation between social movements and the antipsychiatric approach.

GARY: Can you elaborate on the problems between Jean Baudrillard and Félix Guattari? Despite early cooperative efforts in the French Maoist movement, Baudrillard's break with progressive politics and the French Left was early and definitive. Yet Guattari sometimes had favorable things to say about Baudrillard, especially the simulation hypothesis when applied to the first Gulf War. Your acceptance of simulation as deregulation suggests a rapprochement with Baudrillard's legacy is necessary. What are its conditions?

BIFO: The relationship between Baudrillard and Guattari and in a broad sense the difference and the controversy between Baudrillard and Foucault, Deleuze and Guattari, and Lyotard is, I think, a very interesting subject. It's a subject that has never really been confronted, as far as I know.

The friends of Foucault decided never to answer the provocations of Baudrillard, after the publication of *Forget Foucault*. And the second generation of Guattarians (if I may label myself this way, and you, and our friends) have always been embarrassed by this quarrel. I think we absolutely have to go back to the texts, understand the texts in the special situations of the 1970s and of the 1980s. I have tried to do this in *The Soul at Work*. Many pages are dedicated to this confrontation, and I have admitted that Baudrillard, especially in his *Symbolic Exchange and Death*, was been extremely far-sighted.

Having emphasized the ambiguous character of desire, Baudrillard has often been accused of acting as an agent of dissuasion, because of his pessimistic view of the future in consumerist society. Thirty-five years after the publication of *Symbolic Exchange and Death*, I think that this book has to be read together with *Anti-Oedipus* if we want to understand the entire spectrum of the anthropological change that has been produced by capitalism in the age of globalization.

If you only refer to Baudrillard's vision, you miss the energy of subjectivation and the potency of autonomy. But if you read only *Anti-Oedipus* and forget about *Symbolic Exchange and Death*, you refuse to see the dark side of desire, and you risk becoming a fan of neoliberal deregulation and of the false ideology of boundless energy.

NICK: To draw to a close I would like to turn to your more recent political and media practice. You were one of the founders of the Rekombinant mailing list in the early 2000s—can you comment on the purpose of this list, and the reasons for bringing it to an end?

BIFO: In the 1990s, Arthur Kroker and the Critical Art Ensemble used the word "recombinant" in order to define the special feature of technologies like informatics and biogenetics. Following this intuition, with some friends who were activists, artists, psychologists, and biologists, I created a mailing list called Rekombinant.

The list was launched in the highpoint of the movement for global justice, in 2000. It was mainly dedicated to the relation between social activism and the new technologies, and played an important role in discussion about the philosophical and political issues of the movement. The list had 1800 subscribers, most of them Italian researchers, when I and Matteo Pasquinelli (the webmaster, and the main contributor to the list) decided to bring this experience to a close.

We made this decision because we thought that the list was inscribed in the past configuration of the movement, and that it was becoming an obstacle to the creation of something new, something that could adapt to the postactivist phase. As a form of communication and collective research, the mailing list seems to be scarcely in touch with the present of the Web 2.0. Therefore, we are going to start a new virtual space of research and elaboration, which will be mainly dedicated to schizotherapy and politics in the age of disruption, and to poetry as a way to counter the invasive velocity of the image. The new space will be called *Lotremond.*

Conducted by email in Spring 2010

BIBLIOGRAPHY

Akerlof, G. A. and R. J. Shiller. 2009. *Animal Spirits: How Human Psychology Drives the Economy, and Why It Matters for Global Capitalism.* Princeton: Princeton University Press.

Albert, M. 1993. *Capitalism Against Capitalism.* London: Wiley.

Badiou, A. 2008. *The Meaning of Sarkozy.* Translated by D. Fernbach. London: Verso.

Ballard, J. G. 1996. *Cocaine Nights.* London: HarperCollins.

Ballard, J. G. 2000. *Super-Cannes.* New York: Picador.

Baudrillard, J. 1993a. *Symbolic Exchange and Death.* London: Sage.

Baudrillard. J. 1993b. *The Transparency of Evil: Essays on Extreme Phenomena.* Translated by J. Benedict and J. S. Baddeley. London: Verso.

Baudrillard, J. 2003. *The Spirit of Terrorism.* Translated by C. Turner. London: Verso.

Benasayag, M. and G. Schmidt. 2007. *Les passions tristes.* Paris: Editions La Découverte.

Benjamin, W. 1992. "The Work of Art in the Age of Mechanical Reproduction." In *Illuminations.* Edited by H. Arendt. London: Fontana Press.

Berardi, F. 2008. *Félix Guattari: Thought, Friendship and Visionary Cartography.* Translated by G. Mecchia and C. J. Stivale. New York: Palgrave.

Berardi, F. 2009. *Precarious Rhapsody.* London: Minor Compositions, 2009.

Berardi, F. 2009. *The Soul at Work: From Alienation to Autonomy.* Translated by F. Cadel and G. Mecchia. Los Angeles: Semiotext(e).

Boccioni, U., G. Balla, C. Carrà, G. Severini, and L, Russolo. 1970. "Futurist Painting: Technical Manifesto." In *Futurist Manifestos.* Edited by U. Apollonio. Translated by R. Brain. New York: Viking.

Calabrese, O. 1987. *L'età neobarocca.* Bari: Laterza.

Carrol, L. 1971. *Through the Looking-Glass.* London: Nonesuch Press.

Carrère D'Encausse, H. 1998. *Lenin.* Paris: Fayard.

Cooper, M. 2008. *Life as Surplus: Biotechnology and Capitalism in the Neoliberal Era.* Washington: University of Washington Press.

Critical Art Ensemble 1993. *Electronic Disturbance.* New York: Semiotext(e).

Davis, M. 1990. *City of Quartz: Excavating the Future in Los Angeles*. New York: Vintage.

Davis, M. 2003. *Dead Cities and Other Tales*. New York: The New Press.

Deleuze, G. 1988. *Foucault*. Translated by S. Hand. Minneapolis: University of Minnesota Press.

Deleuze, G. 1990. *The Logic of Sense*. Edited by C. V. Boundas. Translated by M. Lester with C. Stivale. New York: Columbia.

Deleuze, G. 1993. *The Fold: Leibniz and the Baroque*. Translated by T. Conley. Minneapolis: University of Minnesota Press.

Deleuze, G. and F. Guattari. 1994. *What is Philosophy?*. Translated by H. Tomlinson and G. Burchell. New York: Columbia University Press.

Drucker, P. 1989. *The New Realities*. New York: Harper and Row.

Echeverria, B. 2006. *Vuelta de siglo*. Mexico DF: Ediciones Era.

Ehrenberg, A. 1998. *La Fatigue d'être soi: dépression et société*. Paris: Editions Odile Jacob.

Formenti, C. 2000. *Incantati dalla Rete*. Cortina.

Formenti, C. 2002. *Mercanti di futuro*. Einaudi.

Formenti, C. 2008. *Cybersoviet*. Cortina.

Foucault, M. 2008. *The Birth of Biopolitics: Lectures at the Collège de France 1978–1979*. Translated by G. Burchell. New York: Palgrave.

Franzen, J. 2001. *The Corrections*. New York: Farrar, Straus and Giroux.

Georgescu-Roegen, N. 1975. "Energy and Economic Myths." *Southern Economic Journal* 413: 347–81.

Gibson, W. 1984. *Neuromancer*. New York: Ace.

Gibson, W. 2003. *Pattern Recognition*. New York: Putnam Publishing.

Goldsen, R. K. 1977. *Show and Tell Machine: How American Television Works and Works You Over*. New York: Doubleday.

Goodman, A. 2009 "Climate Discord: From Hopenhagen to Nopenhagen," *Truthdig*. www.truthdig.com/report/item/climate_discord_from_hopenhagen_to_nopengagen_20091222.

Gorz, A. 1988. *Métamorphoses du travail: Quête du sens, critique de la raison économique*. Paris: Galilée.

Gruzinski, S. 2001. *Images at War: Mexico from Columbus to Blade Runner (1492-2019)*. Translated by H. Maclean. Durham: Duke University Press.

Guattari, F. 1995. *Chaosmosis: An Ethico-Aesthetic Paradigm*. Translated by P. Bains and J. Pefanis. Sydney: Power Publications.

Hegel, G. W. F. 1977. *Phenomenology of Spirit*. Translated by A.V. Miller. Oxford: Claredon Press.

Joll, J. 1960. *Three Intellectuals in Politics*. New York: Pantheon Books.

Kelly, K. 1994. *Out of Control: The New Biology of Machines, Social Systems, and the Economic World*. Reading, Mass.: Addison-Wesley.

Khlebnikov, V. 1987. *Collected Works*, vol. 1. Translated by P. Schmidt, Cambridge. MA: Harvard University Press.

Kristeva, J. 1992. *Black Sun: Depression and Melancholia*. Translated by L. S. Roudiez. New York: Columbia University Press.

Kroker, A. and M. A. Weinstein. 1993. *Data Trash: The Theory of the Virtual Class*. New York: St. Martin's Press.

Lama Anagarika Govinda 1960. *Foundations of Tibetan Mysticism*. London: Weiser Books.

Lévy, P. 1991. *L'Idéographie dynamique*. Paris: La Découverte.

Lovink, G. 2002. *Dark Fiber*. Cambridge, Mass.: MIT Press.

Lyotard, J.–F. 1984. *The Postmodern Condition: A Report on Knowledge*. Translated by G. Bennington and B. Massumi. Minneapolis: University of Minnesota Press.

Marazzi, C. 2010. *The Violence of Financial Capitalism*. Translated by K. Lebedeva. Los Angeles: Semiotetext(e).

Marinetti, F. T. 2004. "To the Racing Car." In *A Selection of Modern Italian Poetry in Translation*. Edited and translated by R. Payne. Montréal: McGill-Queens University Press.

Marx, K. 1973. *Grundrisse: Foundations of the Critique of Political Economy*. Translated by M. Nicolaus. Harmondsworth: Penguin.

Minc, A. and S. Nora. 1981. *The Computerization of Society: A Report to the President of France*. Cambridge, Mass.: MIT Press.

Muraro, L. 1991. *L'ordine simbolico della madre*. Rome: Riuniti.

Pasquinelli, M. 2008. *Animal Spirits: A Bestiary of the Commons*. Rotterdam: NAi Publishers.

Raunig, G. 2007. *Art and Revolution: Transversal Activism in the Long Twentieth Century*. Translated by A. Derieg. Los Angeles: Semiotext(e).

Ripellino, A. M. 1978. "Tentativo di esplorazione del continente Khlebnikov." In *Saggi in forma di ballate*. Torino: Einaudi.

Robin, J. 1989. *Changer d'ère*. Paris: Seuil.

Robin, R. 2007. "Commentary: Learner-Based Listening and Technological Authenticity," *Language Learning and Technology* 11(1): 109–115.

Saviano, R. 2007. *Gomorrah: Italy's Other Mafia*. Translated by V. Jewiss. London: Macmillan.

Schwartz, P. 1993. "Post-Capitalist," *Wired* 1.03, July-August. Available: www.wired.com/wired/archive/1.03/drucker.html

Sennett, R. 1998. *The Corrosion of Character: The Transformation of Work in Modern Capitalism*. New York: WW Norton.

Sordello, R. 1983. "Money and the City," in *Money and the Soul of the World*. Dallas: Pegasus Foundation.

Terranova, T. 2004. *Network Culture: Politics for the Information Age*. Cambridge: Pluto.

Turbulence. 2009. "Life in Limbo?," *Turbulence* 5, available: //turbulence.org.uk/turbulence-5/

Williams, P. 1986. *Only Apparently Real: The World of Philip K. Dick*. Maryland: Arbor House.

Wright, S. 2002. *Storming Heaven: Class Composition and Struggle in Italian Autonomist Marxism*. London: Pluto.

Support AK Press!

AK Press is one of the world's largest and most productive anarchist publishing houses. We're entirely worker-run and

democratically managed. We operate without a corporate structure—no boss, no managers, no bullshit. We publish close to twenty books every year, and distribute thousands of other titles published by other like-minded independent presses from around the globe.

The Friends of AK program is a way that you can directly contribute to the continued existence of AK Press, and ensure that we're able to keep publishing great books just like this one! Friends pay a minimum of $25 per month, for a minimum three month period, into our publishing account. In return, Friends automatically receive (for the duration of their membership), as they appear, one free copy of every new AK Press title. They're also entitled to a 20% discount on everything featured in the AK Press Distribution catalog and on the website, on any and every order. You or your organization can even sponsor an entire book if you should so choose!

There's great stuff in the works—so sign up now to become a Friend of AK Press, and let the presses roll!

Won't you be our friend? Email friendsofak@akpress.org for more info, or visit the Friends of AK Press website:
http://www.akpress.org/programs/friendsofak

Printed in the USA
CPSIA information can be obtained
at www.ICGtesting.com
JSHW012030140824
68134JS00033B/2975

9 781849 350594